The Fun of Growing Forever

By the Author

Liberating Jesus

My Thomas

The Fun of Dying

The Fun of Staying in Touch

The Fun of Growing Forever

The Fun of Living Together

The Fun of Meeting Jesus

(Children's Picture-Book)

The Fun of Growing Forever

We Can't Transform the World Until We Transform Ourselves

Roberta Grimes

Copyright © 2016, 2021 by Roberta Grimes. All rights reserved.

You may make copies of this text for any purpose that helps you or humankind develop spiritually. Don't charge money for anything in this book. Give it away freely. Please put the name of the book, its copyright, and the series website (www.RobertaGrimes.com) on the first page of any copies you make so people can keep in contact with us as we add to the knowledge we're trying to bring to humankind.

Otherwise, no part of this book may be reproduced in any written, electronic, photocopied, or other media without written permission of the publisher or author. The exception is in the case of brief quotations embodied in critical articles or reviews and pages where permission is specifically granted by the publisher or author.

"Scripture quotations taken from the New American Standard Bible®, Copyright © 1960, 1962, 1963, 1968, 1971, 1972, 1973, 1975, 1977, 1995 by The Lockman Foundation Used by permission." (www.Lockman.org)

Paperback ISBN: 978-1-7374106-4-5
ePub ISBN: 978-1-7374106-5-2

GR

Greater Reality Publications
23 Payne Place
Normal, IL 61761
www.greaterreality.com
800 690-4232

Contact the Author: www.robertagrimes.com

This book is gratefully dedicated to each of the thousands of unsung scholars whose wonderful work made it possible.

Table of Contents

Foreword by Jack Canfield i

Introduction 1

The Time for Transformation is Now

Chapter One: The Dead Tell Us What Really Is Going On 9

Chapter Two: The Purpose of Your Life is Spiritual Growth 15

Chapter Three: Religions Can Be of Little Help 25

Chapter Four: Spiritual Growth Consists in Remembering Who You Are 29

Spiritual Growth Made Simple

Chapter Five: It is up to You and Me to Transform the World 39

Chapter Six: An Attitude of Gratitude 49

Chapter Seven: Universal Forgiveness 57

Chapter Eight: Universal Love 73

Chapter Nine: Driving is a Wonderful Spiritual Exercise 91

Chapter Ten: Your Life and the World are About to Change 97

Appendices

Appendix I: Brief Suggested Study Guide 107

Appendix II: References List 111

Appendix III: Listening to Jesus 145

Appendix IV: A Brief Overview of the Afterlife Evidence 163

Appendix V: A Brief Overview of the Greater Reality 169

Appendix VI: Experiences of Light 175

Foreword
by Jack Canfield

Roberta Grimes is a business attorney who spent decades figuring out where the dead are now, and then she did something important. She sat at their feet and asked them why it is that we even are here at all. The answer they gave her led her to attempt to live the Gospel teachings of Jesus Christ, and then led her to announce in this book that not only have we at last discovered the meaning and purpose of human life, but buried deep in the Christian Bible are what may be the simplest and most transformative spiritual teachings ever found. Roberta calls it tragic that more Christians aren't following the teachings of Jesus. She tells us that his teachings, when followed, actually transform us internally, and she shares the enticing suggestion that if even as few as ten percent of us will fully live the teachings of the Gospels, we can begin an era of universal peace and understanding over all the earth.

    The reason why we can transform the world if enough of us will transform ourselves is tied to a dawning understanding that reality is consciousness-based. Quantum physicist Max Planck discovered a century ago that matter arises from consciousness, and that, as he put it, "mind is the matrix of all matter." We are learning now that consciousness exists in a vibratory range, of which the highest vibration is love and the lowest is fear. Roberta plausibly claims that the rise of fear and hatred on earth is our fundamental problem, so for enough of us to instead choose love is our best solution to the world's problems.

That being the case, how can we help as many people as possible to raise their spiritual vibration away from fear and toward more perfect love? What Roberta calls "those we used to think were dead" have told her that the answer lies in the Gospel teachings of Jesus. What a liberating thought! I believe that humankind's greatest need is unconditional love and equality, and Jesus Christ exemplified both these qualities. But before Roberta would recommend his teachings to others, she first set out to try them herself.

Watching her attempt to do what she claims that few people have ever really done—actually live the teachings of Jesus—makes for a light and enjoyable read. Watching her arrive at a spiritual place that she had never imagined existed is heart-lifting. She claims now that the teachings of Jesus are a system that works by helping us remember the spiritual perfection that already is ours, so we really aren't learning anything new. We are just revealing it to ourself. Watching her so easily accomplish what should be and can be natural in all our lives makes you realize just how off-track we have become. No wonder so much of our civilization is a mess!

Roberta begins with gratitude, which she says must come first. I tell people that what you think about and thank about, is what you will bring about, and she echoes that point. As Meister Ekhart Tolle has said, "If the only prayer you ever say in your entire life is thank you, it will be enough." Roberta insists, however, that gratitude is just the indispensable beginning.

Next she tackles forgiveness, which I also agree is essential for spiritual growth. As she says, forgiving others is something

Foreward

that we do for ourselves! Resentment is like drinking poison and hoping your enemies will die. Quite the opposite, it slowly kills you. You cannot control the economy, the government, or anything else that is external, but you can control how you respond to these things; and if your habitual response becomes love and peace and not fear and resentment, you can totally transform your mind. Thankfully, she then shares a method for learning to forgive everything once and for all. It's powerful, yet simple to do ... and it works.

Roberta claims that we cannot even love in a way that transforms us spiritually until we have learned universal forgiveness, but once we are forgiving at that level then love comes as naturally to us as breathing. She tells us that it is this automatic, instinctive love for each person on the face of the earth that truly raises us spiritually. In my view, our whole wellbeing is dependent on our expressing love. It is not about what comes back; it is about what goes out! Love is a force more formidable than any other. It is powerful enough to transform you in a moment, and it offers you more joy than any material possessions ever could.

As Albert Einstein said, "The world as we have created it is a process of our thinking. It cannot be changed without changing our thinking." Ultimately our salvation comes when we begin to think more loving thoughts—thoughts that transcend fear. Since everything you want in life lies on the other side of fear, and nothing is going to change until you change, now is the time to transform your life; and as you do, you also begin for all the world the long-delayed advent of universal love, kindness, and perpetual peace.

One individual can begin a movement that turns the tide of history. Martin Luther King in the civil rights movement, Mohandas Gandhi in India, and Nelson Mandela in South Africa are examples of people standing up with courage and non-violence to bring about needed changes. Roberta Grimes is telling us now that the transformation that has become essential to the future of humankind was begun two thousand years ago by the greatest individual of them all. And now it is up to each of us to stand up and embody that transformation. The future of the world is up to us. The path is clear; we just need to walk it.

Jack Canfield is an internationally recognized leader in the field of personal development, and the beloved originator of the Chicken Soup for the Soul series. He is the author or co-author of more than 150 books, including 66 best-sellers, with more than 100 million copies in print in 47 languages. In 2014, Success magazine named him **"One of the most influential leaders in personal growth and achievement."**

Introduction

"What I have seen is the totality recapitulated as One ... It is just as if you lit a flame from a live flame: It is the entire flame you receive."

—St. Symeon, Christian mystic (949–1022)

"Do not store up for yourselves treasures on earth, where moth and rust destroy, and where thieves break in and steal. But store up for yourselves treasures in heaven, where neither moth nor rust destroys, and where thieves do not break in or steal; for where your treasure is, there your heart will be also."

—Jesus (MT 6:19–21)

"If you want to awaken all of humanity, then awaken all of yourself. If you want to eliminate the suffering in the world, then eliminate all that is dark and negative in yourself. Truly, the greatest gift you have to give is that of your own self-transformation."

—Lao Tsu, Chinese philosopher
(sixth century BC)

"Someday, after mastering the winds, the waves, the tides and gravity, we shall harness for God the energies of love, and then, for a second time in the history of the world, man will have discovered fire."

—Pierre Teilhard de Chardin,
French Jesuit Priest (1881–1955)

Two childhood experiences of light that I describe for you in Appendix VI led me to spend almost half a century in the enjoyable study of death. There is a lot of good information available about what happens at and after death that is so consistent and complete that our survival of death can no longer be reasonably doubted. If my saying that surprises you, then in order for you to make sense of this book you may first need to educate yourself! Appendix IV is a brief overview of the various kinds of afterlife evidence, while Appendix V is a quick summary of what is now known about the greater reality that we reenter at death. For more in-depth reading, Appendices I and II are lists of suggested resources.

What afterlife researchers have discovered turns out to be a great deal more than just the fact that human minds are eternal! **Afterlife studies is a genuine science that encompasses a consciousness-based reality many times the size of this material universe.** The physics of consciousness and all its implications will so dominate the second half of this century that eventually people will look back on today's benighted scientific beliefs very much as we now look back on the practice of balancing humors by bleeding the sick. Revelations to come over the next few decades are going to change everything.

Perhaps the most important insight to flow from what the dead are telling us is that now, quite unexpectedly, we have received the answer to humankind's oldest question. At last we know why we are here!

You came into this lifetime eager to achieve the greatest possible spiritual growth. That is what the dead tell us is the reason why we even are born. As best we have been able to determine, it is the reason why the universe exists. And the fact that you have not always known this is the greatest indictment of mainstream science and organized religions that I can imagine.

We all seek meaning in our lives, especially as we move past the grubbing for money and status of our early years. And even those who find earthly success soon discover that there is no end to those struggles, no top to be found, no rat-race prize, so every thoughtful person eventually sees that whatever success we might find on earth gives us nothing more than toys whose luster is going to dim as our bodies fail. No matter how rich and famous we become, we realize in the end that we have never owned anything.

The only thing that you and I can own is the powers of our eternal minds, so achieving spiritual growth while on earth is the best way to add to our permanent wealth. Perhaps the notion of growing spiritually doesn't seem appealing to you now. It sounds stuffy and churchy. Who needs that? Fine. Then let's call it plainly what it is: spiritual growth means ever more perfect love. Most of us would say that love feels good, but on Earth love is as ephemeral as mist. Perhaps if you were aware that spiritual growth means feeling ever more deeply in love all the time, with everyone and everything forevermore, you might find the concept more attractive.

Achieving spiritual growth turns out to be the whole secret to human happiness. This is true for all of us, whether rich or poor and no matter how much fun we might seem to be having. Since we have not known why we were here, we have been seeking happiness in all the wrong places; but thanks to insights lately received from people we used to think were dead, our floundering is about to end. And what we are learning now about the spiritual growth that is our core human need is remarkable:

- **Growing spiritually has nothing to do with religions.** In fact, as you will see, religious practices can impede or even prevent spiritual growth.
- **Growing spiritually is amazingly easy!** You can make it a part of your daily life without much affecting your routines, and almost from the start it feels delicious. It doesn't take long to make lots of progress, so it never is too late to begin.
- **Growing spiritually makes you happier.** Whatever else may be going on in your life, elevating your personal spiritual energy makes coping easier. It makes everything look brighter.
- **Growing spiritually can bring you a much better afterlife experience.** The heavens that we enter at death turn out to be a spiritual hierarchy in which those who are more developed spiritually will have much richer eternal lives. Since you are here and living this earth-life anyway, why not use whatever time you have left to make your eternal life more wonderful?

The reasons why all these things are true will very soon be clear to you. For now, only know that spiritual growth is easy, it makes you happy, and there is good evidence that it is the reason why you were born. It doesn't even take long to achieve, once you put your mind to it, so it never is too late to start. And if improving your own happiness both here and hereafter is not inducement enough for you to want to feed the craving for spiritual growth that first brought you here, there is one more important reason why we all should begin this process now.

Human civilization is on a course to disaster. Those that we used to think were dead are telling us that unless we act now, in two hundred years a war will begin that will make this planet unlivable. On the other hand, if sufficient people will begin now to develop spiritually, our future in two hundred years will be a literal heaven on earth. They present our alternatives as just that stark.

Of course, some who are reading these words will shrug. In two hundred years we'll all be dead! But those who are dead now tell us that our downward course over two hundred years will be an awful acceleration of the troubling trends that we see around us now. So for people who care about the grandchildren that our own grandchildren will hold in their arms, the stakes in this could not be higher.

This book is a course in spiritual growth made simple. Very simple! To grow spiritually, you will not need to learn to meditate, chant, pray, or do yoga; you won't need to find a guru, go to church, take expensive courses, join a cult, change your diet, or even give up drinking. Most of us have neither the time nor the interest to do much more than live our lives, so this course meets us where we are now and leads us in transforming ourselves from within. At one time I thought the amazing way this works must be a literal miracle; but then I figured out why it works. Now I only wonder how humankind can have been so clueless for so long.

The course I am recommending to you is not the only one that you might choose, but I think it is the easiest to follow and probably the most effective. These teachings are a philosophy based in your own essential nature, and they work not by teaching you anything new, but rather by helping you remember who you are.

Few Christians follow the teachings of Jesus. They see them as optional in view of the fact that they believe Jesus was born to die for our sins. Indeed, many Christians have paid so little attention to the Gospel teachings that they have sullied the name of Jesus by the way they have treated other people. Please understand that their behavior has nothing to do with the genuine Jesus! But if reading his name here bothers you, simply obscure the Biblical references and turn his words into nothing more than proven wisdom that has no source.

It never is too late to begin! Give yourself the gift of spiritual growth, make the very most that you can of your life, and together we will transform the world.

The Time for Transformation is Now

Chapter One
The Dead Tell Us What Really Is Going On

"I do not feel obliged to believe that the same God who has endowed us with sense, reason, and intellect has intended us to forgo their use."

—Galileo Galilei, Italian philosopher (1564–1642)

"New opinions are always suspected, and usually opposed, without any other reason but because they are not already common."

—John Locke, English Enlightenment philosopher and physician (1632–1704)

"Concerning matter, we have been all wrong. What we have called matter is energy, whose vibration has been so lowered as to be perceptible to the senses. There is no matter."

—Albert Einstein, winner of the 1921 Nobel Prize in Physics (1879–1955)

"Nothing real can be threatened. Nothing unreal exists. Herein lies the peace of God."

—*A Course in Miracles* (Introduction)

"The day science begins to study non-physical phenomena, it will make more progress in one decade than in all the previous centuries of its existence."

—Nikola Tesla, Serbian-American Physicist, Inventor and Engineer (1856–1943)

The dead know a great deal more than we do. From their elevated eternal perspective, those of the dead who are better developed can not only tell us why we are here, but they also seem to be able to "game out" and predict from present trends our likely future. So if you are not yet certain that we survive our deaths, then please begin to educate yourself! I don't know how important knowledge of the afterlife is to your rapid spiritual growth, but I strongly suspect that it helps. The truth frees us from fear and superstitions, and knowing how much your degree of spiritual development will matter after you die is going to inspire you to want to grow spiritually. But if your time is tight, then simply assume that afterlife researchers have it right, and fill in the gaps in your knowledge later.

The higher-level dead who communicate with us are telling us a great deal more than just the fact that human minds are eternal. What afterlife researchers have begun to glimpse is a greater reality that is many times the size of this whole physical universe, complex and astounding and based in love. And insofar as we are able to determine, all of it is governed by consciousness.

What the Dead are Telling Us Now

Here are a few important facts that the dead consistently share:

- **The only thing that is real is an infinitely powerful energy-like potentiality without size or form, alive in the sense that your mind is alive, highly emotional and therefore probably self-aware.** Everything else that we believe is real is an artifact of that potentiality. Credit for the scientific discovery of the base consciousness energy that the dead describe goes to physicist Max Planck, who referred to it as "Mind." We might with justification now shout "Eureka!" and begin to call this base energy "God," but it bears little resemblance to the Christian God. We can find no human-like God that feels anger or jealousy or the need to judge us. The consciousness energy that is all that exists is in its pure essence perfect love.

- **All human minds are part of the base energy that is all that exists.** Not as separate dots, mind you, but rather as inextricable parts of one whole. In other words, each of our minds is part of God, and apparently we never leave God. Hold this thought, since it is going to be essential to your understanding of why these teachings work, and how they can transform the world.

- **We come into lives on earth in order to experience negativity here so we can better grow spiritually.** Afterlife researchers are coming to suspect that this universe and the greater reality that includes it are nothing more than a school that is meant to aid our spiritual growth. This concept does present problems, of course, which challenge our limited understanding. If God is perfect, and if our minds are part of God, then why are we not already perfect? In Chapter Four I will give you what I think are the best—if greatly simplified—answers to what is a complex and perplexing question.

Here are two further facts that might make you more comfortable with following these teachings:

- **There is almost no religion practiced in the afterlife levels.** I hedge this statement only because a few might sing hymns for nostalgia's sake. And those who have died too certain about their afterlife beliefs can find that their powerful minds have put them into illusory heavens that look like what they expected to find, but from which they will later have to be rescued. But just as there are no atheists in heaven, so also there are no religionists. People don't need faith when they live in certainty.
- **Jesus is much more important in the afterlife levels than he is here.** They call him the Master. And he is everywhere, teaching and comforting and visiting the children's villages. He is a powerful spiritual center, loved and revered more than you can imagine. The Buddha also is sometimes reported, but he is not seen as comparable to Jesus. In fact, there is some evidence that the Master may be the most advanced being in every dimension and in every universe. He is above all.

A Few Words About God

It is ironic that advocates of scientific inquiry and advocates of religious worship have battled one another for centuries about which view of reality will prevail, when in truth neither of them has it right. The human-like Christian God that feels anger and jealousy does not exist. Instead, the only thing that exists is an infinitely loving Power that continuously gives rise to everything else. Which means that scientists who still want to think that reality is random are off-track, too. Indeed, scientific inquiry has been in the weeds for all of the hundred years since Max Planck first realized that consciousness is primary.

Dr. Planck called the base consciousness Mind, but as I try to help you become more comfortable with what we now know to be true I will refer to it here as God. You might think of Mind as the modern, enlightened, improved and much more wonderful version of what God always has been, although thousands of years ago people could not have understood the true nature of the genuine God.

So if you are an atheist, please be assured that the human-like version of God does not exist. If you are religious, you can come home with joy to the certainty that God is all-powerful love, and that you are God's best-beloved child.

The Afterlife Evidence Affirms the Teachings of Jesus

Without the testimony of the dead, we would not be able to confirm that the Gospel words of Jesus are true. Two thousand years ago, Jesus told us things about God, reality, death, the afterlife, and the meaning and purpose of our lives that we could not have validated by any means until we first had put together a thorough account of what the dead are telling us, which happened late in the twentieth century.

In Appendix III, I outline some of the astonishing correspondences between what Jesus said two thousand years ago and what the dead are telling us now. Given the difficult road that the teachings of Jesus have had to travel in order to be with us at all, even garbled, the fact that they turn out to be so consistent with an independent, verifiable source of information may eventually be seen to amount to nothing less than a new revelation from God.

So we begin this adventure in spiritual growth and learning ever more perfect love with the great advantage of understandings that were not available to previous generations. As you read, you may find yourself nursing a growing indignation at Christianity, which has always held the truth in its Bible while it taught its faithful something else. But I hope you will instead begin to feel gratitude toward Christianity as the custodian of teachings that could not have been preserved for us in any other way. Thank you, Paul, for protecting these teachings by enclosing them in first-century Judaism! Thank you, beautiful Christian martyrs, who died to ensure that the truth might live! And thank you, beloved modern Christians, that you still tend the Master's flame of truth even if you may not choose to live by it yourselves. Thank you!

Finally, after two thousand years and because Christianity has preserved it for us, now at last it is time for us to open humankind's ultimate gift.

Chapter Two
The Purpose of Your Life is Spiritual Growth

"The greatest among you shall be your servant. Whoever exalts himself shall be humbled; and whoever humbles himself shall be exalted."

—Jesus (MT 23:11–12)

"Permit the children to come to Me; do not hinder them; for the kingdom of God belongs to such as these. Truly I say to you, whoever does not receive the kingdom of God like a child will not enter it at all."

—Jesus (MK 10:14–15)

"Blessed are the poor in spirit, for theirs is the kingdom of heaven. Blessed are those who mourn, for they shall be comforted. Blessed are the gentle, for they shall inherit the earth. Blessed are those who hunger and thirst for righteousness, for they shall be satisfied. Blessed are the merciful, for they shall receive mercy. Blessed are the pure in heart, for they shall see God."

—Jesus (MT 5:1–8)

Usually the quotations at the starts of chapters are there for your enjoyment, but in this case the quotations are this chapter's message. Please read them again, while knowing that every one of them was spoken by Jesus and preserved for us in the Christian Gospels. And the dead now confirm for us that every one of them is true.

The Meaning and Purpose of Human Life

It seems strange that it has taken so long for humankind to figure out why we are here. Wouldn't you think this is the sort of thing that we would have known all along? The fact that science remains materialist in the face of evidence that nothing is solid is certainly a factor in our ongoing ignorance, and of course religions are limited to giving us answers based just in their own dogmas. When we Google the question, we are left to chew on some imaginative but unsatisfying ideas.

Fortunately, in the twenty-first century we are receiving detailed information from people who are in a position to know. Simply dying does not bring enlightenment! After death, we remain essentially the same people we were before we died, but we have ready access to more of our minds (what you might call our "superconsciousness"). And we live in a place where questions can be answered by more advanced beings whose knowledge far exceeds our own. So now, for the first time since our ancestors first risked walking on two legs, we know the reason why you and I are here. Imagine a drum-roll ...

We are here to accomplish more rapid spiritual growth.

That is it, and that is all. It turns out that life in the afterlife levels is like lying around on a spiritual couch, while coming to earth is the rough equivalent of an hour or two in a spiritual gym. Each negative thing that happens to us here—each contentious marriage or loss of a child; each health issue, job issue, fight with a friend—each horrible thing is nothing worse than a gym-machine designed to help us strengthen a particular set of spiritual muscles. We eagerly plan our lives to be full of the very pains that we are certain must mean there can be no God who loves us. True, it is not much fun to be here! But neither is it fun to go to the gym. We come to earth because there is no way in heaven that we can so easily do what those who live there tell us they all crave to do: there is no more rapid way for us to grow spiritually than to enter an earth-lifetime.

So, what is spiritual growth, anyway? The words sound like fluff-words. Religious. New-Agey. Might they have a meaning on which everybody would agree? When I Googled the term, most definitions were religious. The most common definition in the West is that spiritual growth consists in becoming more like Jesus Christ.

Well, okay. But, again, what does that mean? Jesus had no need to grow, so how can we become more like him when we are starting out so far behind him? And what does "more like Jesus" even mean? When we take this definition apart, it looks like just more fluff.

Neither Science nor Christianity Can Help Us to Understand Spiritual Growth

The reason why our two most trusted institutions cannot tell us why we are here, and neither can help us define spiritual growth, is that it never occurs to practitioners in either field that these are questions that should be answered. Mainstream science considers our minds to be artifacts of meat-brains that will die, so for us to grow spiritually while in bodies would be useless. And mainstream Christianity assures us that since Jesus died to redeem us from God's judgment, we are certain to get into heaven. We don't have to do anything beyond claiming Jesus as our personal savior, and in some denominations even people who have fallen far from any sort of standard can do that and be "saved" on their deathbeds.

With both science and Christianity incapable of defining spiritual growth for us, we must turn again to the dead, and to the Master. It turns out that they do agree on a definition for spiritual growth; but for us to understand it, we first will need to better understand what we will here call the physics of consciousness.

Reality is Based in Consciousness

The physics of all of reality is governed by what we think of as human-like consciousness. The prevalence of consciousness is less obvious to us while we are here on earth, since the physics of this material universe has a mathematics-based overlay of what we might call Newtonian physics. Afterlife researchers assume that a more restrictive physics applies in this universe to keep us from using our powerful minds to

The Purpose of Your Life is Spiritual Growth

cheat on our spiritual lessons, but the reason for it doesn't matter. Even in this physical universe, consciousness is fundamental. And in most of reality—including in the places where the dead reside—consciousness plainly governs everything. All that we now think of as real is part of something like a thought, which fact has manifold and profound implications.

I am going to give you here a quick explanation of what afterlife researchers have come to understand is true of the foundational consciousness, and therefore why what the Master and the dead agree is the purpose of our lives makes sense. It all makes sense! And it is so simple.

You will recall from Chapter One that the only thing that exists is an infinitely powerful energy-like potentiality that we experience as consciousness. All our minds are inextricably part of it. This potentiality is intensely emotional, and its emotions are at a range of vibratory rates from low-vibration emotions like fear, hatred, anger and grief to the highest emotional vibration, which of course is perfect love. (If reading the L-word makes you wince, you might prefer to think of the highest emotional vibration as just "consciousness's affinity for itself.") The more loving consciousness is, the more powerful it is, so at its Source its power is infinite. The less loving consciousness is, the weaker it is, so the most evil entities are effectively helpless.

If you are having trouble getting your mind around the effect that emotions have on consciousness, you might try re-experiencing the vibrational range of emotions for yourself. First, call up the beautiful faces of all the people you love most. Let their presence and the wonder of who they are fill your mind and heart, and know that the way the thought of those you love lifts you is a taste of the highest-vibration spiritual energy. Then, once you have recalled what love feels like, give yourself a little dose of fear. I hate asking you to do this, since it feels as if I am asking you to dive into filth; but just for an instant, call into your mind whatever are your own greatest fears. Let them consume you. Add to them whatever low-vibration emotions you might lately have nursed, whether anger or hatred, grief or resentment, and feature in your mind the faces of the people who inspired these negative emotions in you. Are you there? Sorry. That hollow, panicky flutter and the icky way you are feeling now is very low consciousness vibration. It is what governs the twenty-first-century world. Feel it, then very quickly think of puppies and kittens and sunshine!

What is possible for you is nothing less than choosing to experience forevermore only the spiritual vibration of love. Always. No matter what might be happening. You can banish from your mind eternally not only fear, but also every other feeling that you might experience as a downer. This is what you came here to learn to do. And it is easy! It can be forever. What more can I say to convince you that your doing this now is worth the effort?

Better Understanding the Process of Spiritual Growth

For each of us to have and to exercise free will is essential. If we cannot also choose fear and hatred, then our making a loving choice means nothing, so our freedom to choose negative emotions is part of the spiritual-growth package with which we entered these bodies. Of course, for us to choose any negative emotion has consequences that go far beyond whether we are making ourselves unhappy, as you will shortly see; but for now, only know that since apparently we cannot grow spiritually without free will, we all have it, whether or not we are aware of using it.

We come into these bodies with limited minds designed for rapid spiritual learning. Free will is just a part of it! Our eternal minds are far more powerful than the dim awareness that we can access while here, and in fact we leave behind in the afterlife levels as much as eighty percent of who we are. We come to earth with just enough awareness to enable our rapid spiritual growth, very much as you might put on gym clothes to make your concentration on your workout easier. Then, soon after we return home, we reconnect with our greater minds and reassume all the powers and memories that we left behind.

These minimized earth-minds have three traits that can make our spiritual growth much easier. In fact, without these traits in place, for us to learn anything would be a harder slog:

1. **Our earth-minds are lazy.** They don't hum along like a computer, but rather they casually flow like water. They find the easiest course and take it.
2. **Our earth-minds quickly adapt.** So if we rearrange whatever used to be their easiest course, they will take the new route without hesitation.
3. **Our earth-minds operate mostly by habit.** If this were not so, we would have to spend our days repeatedly thinking through how best to open a door or start a

car or take a step or compose a sentence. We would have no mind-space left for anything else.

The fact that our limited earth-minds are *lazy, adaptable,* and *ruled by habits* turns out to be an important key to our achieving rapid spiritual growth.

But what is spiritual growth, anyway?

Since love is the highest consciousness vibration, spiritual growth must be in its essence the achievement of an ever-greater capacity to love perfectly. As Jesus says, **"You are to be perfect, as your heavenly Father is perfect"** (MT 5:48).

Jesus also tells us why our spiritual perfection will be important once we get to the afterlife levels. To take his own words from the Gospel quotations at the start of this chapter:

"The greatest among you shall be your servant." "Whoever does not receive the kingdom of God like a child will not enter it at all."

"Blessed are the poor in spirit, for theirs is the kingdom of heaven."

"Blessed are the gentle, for they shall inherit the earth."

"Blessed are the pure in heart, for they shall see God."

The most spiritually developed people I know are so reminiscent of these words! They are mild, good-humored, and internally secure. They never get angry or express disappointment. When someone antagonizes them, they withdraw. None of them seems to care about money, status, or often even their own basic needs. And they are happy! The happiest people on earth are those who are the most spiritually developed. They are deeply joyous every day, with no need for a reason and no matter what happens.

It may not be necessary for me to add that those on the upper levels of the afterlife live in a state of constant bliss. The very air that they breathe is joy. The greatest pleasures on earth cannot compare! There even is a body-melding thing that they can do with anyone that produces what they say feels like a whole-body orgasm. I swear!

As you will see in the second part of this book, the process of growing spiritually requires some specific actions on your part, and it is important that they be taken in order. But those actions are simple, and for the most part natural, and they can begin to be effective within weeks. **You can give yourself so much happiness! And what may be almost as important to you is the fact that at last you yourself can take on behalf of everyone on earth your own essential step toward the elevation of human consciousness that is going to save this world from destruction.**

Chapter Three
Religions Can Be of Little Help

"Belief in a cruel God makes a cruel man."

—Thomas Paine, English-American Political Activist (1737–1809)

"Men never do evil so completely and cheerfully as when they do it from religious conviction."

—Blaise Pascal, French physicist and Christian philosopher (1623–1662)

"Man will never be free until the last king is strangled with the entrails of the last priest."

—Denis Diderot, French Enlightenment philosopher (1713–1784)

"All great truths begin as blasphemies."

—George Bernard Shaw, Irish playwright (1856–1950)

"A sense of separation from God is the only lack you really need correct."

—*A Course in Miracles* (VI.2.1)

Although we associate religions with spirituality, and although the easiest set of teachings for making rapid spiritual progress can be found in the Christian Bible, Christianity and other religions can be of little help when we set out to grow spiritually. If you doubt that fact, just look around you! Over the past sixteen hundred years we have made considerable technological progress, medical progress, even political and literary progress. Christianity, however, has not progressed at all in any meaningful way, and nor does it seem to be the case that most Christians in later life are much better developed spiritually than are those who have lived their lives as atheists. Indeed, an excellent case can be made that religions in general can foster some of the very emotions associated with the lowest levels of spiritual development.

The Problems with Religions

All religions suffer from the same issues to a greater or a lesser degree, so I think it may be safe to say that there is no religion on the face of the earth that can help us much when we are trying to grow spiritually. Here is why:

- **No religion puts spiritual growth first.** That is not what religions are about. This might seem counterintuitive at first, but read on.
- **Religions are based in dogmas.** Every religion has a set of beliefs to which its adherents must subscribe or they risk being branded heretics. Freedom of mind is frowned upon by most religious denominations, and it even can be a cause for punishment. Yet for an un-free mind to grow spiritually is impossible.

- **Religions manage their followers with rules.** When it comes to achieving spiritual growth, rules of conduct turn out to be useless, yet rules are the way that nearly all religions attempt to manage our minds. Real spiritual growth is something that must transform us from within; yet even if we obey every Christian rule for our entire lives, we won't be transformed. This difference is crucial!
- **Religious practice can feel good, but it doesn't change our hearts.** For example, Catholicism places great store in the presence of the faithful at Mass, which is a ceremony meant to transform wine and bread into the blood and flesh of Jesus so we can consume it. Even writing that sentence makes me wince! Yet I have participated in many hundreds of Masses, have prayerfully accepted the Host, and have felt better for it. I realize now that what it did for me was to make me feel safe, protected, purer, more virtuous, and just a whole quantum closer to God than all those other people who never went to Mass. This private good-feeling that comes from having participated in religious rituals is the very antithesis of spiritual growth.
- **Religions insert themselves between us and God.** This may be the greatest problem we face as religious people who want to grow spiritually. Since your mind already is inextricably part of the fundamental consciousness energy that religions call God, for anything to come between you and God will make your spiritual development much harder.

And there is one more overriding problem that might even trump all the rest:

- **Religions are based in fear.** This is certainly true of Christianity, where "God-fearing" is thought to be a compliment; and, insofar as I have seen, it is true of all other religions as well. Religions survive by creating in people a great fear—usually a fear of God—and then by providing an antidote to that fear that is available to the faithful if they will follow certain practices. Fear is the deepest and most intractable low-energy emotion. It is the literal opposite of love, so it is impossible for us to love what we fear. Adhering to a belief-system that fosters fear is going to make your spiritual growth not only more difficult, but likely impossible.

Since religions cannot be of much help to us, it is fortunate indeed that we don't need them! From now on, think of spiritual growth not as something that happens mostly on Sundays, but rather as a way of living that permeates every aspect of your life and transforms all that you think and do in ways that are more profound and joyous than you can possibly imagine now. **Spiritual growth means a richer and more abundant life.**

Chapter Four
Spiritual Growth Consists in Remembering Who You Are

"All truths are easy to understand once they are discovered; the point is to discover them."

—Galileo Galilei, Italian philosopher (1564–1642)

"All fear is ultimately reducible to the basic misperception that you have the ability to usurp the power of God."

—A Course in Miracles (II.I.4.1)

"The kingdom of God is not coming with signs to be observed; nor will they say, 'Look, here it is!' or, 'There it is!' For behold, the kingdom of God is within you."

—Jesus (LK 17:21)

"God is spirit, and those who worship Him must worship in spirit and in truth."

—Jesus (JN 4:24)

"It is the Spirit who gives life; the flesh profits nothing; the words that I have spoken to you are spirit and are life."

—Jesus (JN 6:63)

"I came that they may have life, and have it abundantly."

—Jesus (JN 10:10)

Growing spiritually turns out to be amazingly easy. Closely following the Gospel teachings begins a cycle of ever-greater peace and joy and exultant love, and a life no longer troubled by fear or by any other negative thought. Living the teachings is a particular happiness, not dependent on anything external. I was already old when I began to take the teachings of Jesus as seriously as he means them to be taken, but after only five years of living them I cannot even recall the way I felt before.

The Teachings of Jesus Fit Western Lifestyles

Eastern religions put more emphasis on spiritual growth, which is a reason why aspects of Eastern religious practice are spreading in Western countries. I know people who swear that they benefit from meditation, yoga, energy medicine, out-of-body travel, altered states of consciousness, and other exotic-seeming spiritual notions. The spread of these ideas is encouraging, but for most in the West they will not be enough. Here is why:

- **Eastern practices take time and effort to learn.** Most of us find our lives already so full of things that we must do that trying to add a lot of study, meditation, yoga, doing pilgrimages, and perhaps even following a guru or yogi simply won't work for us.
- **Eastern spiritual theories and practices seem strange to many people in the West.** Even having surveyed Eastern religions in college, and having later learned a lot about the greater reality in which they operate, to this day I find them uncomfortably foreign.

- **Many people with Christian backgrounds are afraid to practice another religion.** Christianity is so deeply based in fear of a judgmental God that even those who have fallen away from its practice can suffer some squeamish worries about getting on God's bad side.

The teachings of Jesus solve all of these problems. They come right from the Christian Bible! What could be safer to try than that? They require no special training, no meditation or gurus or chanting, really nothing foreign-seeming at all. Perhaps most importantly, it is easy to make them integral to our daily lives. And they work fast! I began to notice positive changes in myself within weeks.

Given that the teachings of Jesus have always been part of the Christian Bible, the fact that so few people realize that they are a coherent system that works beautifully in fostering our spiritual growth is surprising. How is it possible that we are only now discovering this life-transforming and world-saving gift? A study of church history suggests that during its first millennium, Christianity was producing many more people who took the teachings of Jesus as seriously as he means them to be taken. We know some of those folks now as martyrs and saints. But long ago, Christianity narrowed its primary focus to the notion that Jesus had come to be sacrificed so God will forgive us. For centuries, his Gospel words have been seen by the faithful as just nice suggestions.

The Teachings of Jesus Help Us to Remember Who and What We Are

The Gospel teachings are a process. It's important that they be emphasized in order, and I have found some tricks that make what are already easy teachings even easier and more effective. Within no more than a couple of months, I felt quite different internally. I was more peaceful, somehow softer, more willing to accept and to let things be, and I wasn't anymore reacting to things that used to drive me up the wall. I began to feel inexplicably more content, more delighted with the smallest things, more prone to feeling unexpectedly joyous. And I was really loving people! One of the first big things I noticed was this extraordinary new love for strangers.

It is only in recent months that I have begun to wonder why this transformation in every aspect of my life has been so laughably simple. Learning something new is difficult, especially when you are already old. But when I decided to follow the Gospel teachings, I found myself within weeks beginning a benevolent cycle of internal transformation. I wondered briefly how this was possible. Then I grasped what has to be the answer.

In applying the Gospel teachings of Jesus, we are not learning anything new. We are instead undertaking a process of remembering who and what we already are. Each of us is inextricably part of an infinitely powerful God, already spiritually perfect ourselves, and with nothing more to be learned! Without realizing it, though, each of us is mired in false beliefs about the world, and especially in false beliefs about ourselves. We are told by Christianity that we are sinful and fallen, by science that we are mortal accidents of nature, and by those around us and by our culture that we are defective and even venal. But the teachings of Jesus melt away those beliefs as they ever more clearly reveal to us our true and eternally perfect selves. Spiritual growth is a process of joyfully remembering who and what we already are.

Why Do We Even Need to Grow Spiritually?

If you wonder why our spiritual growth is necessary when we are already part of God, please know that a lot of us wonder about that. There are only two proposed explanations that make any kind of sense to me, but neither really feels conclusive and it may be that neither of them is right:

1. **God may be using us to experience Its creation.** This theory is often proposed, but it raises some important questions. Why isn't the fact that everything is happening within God already sufficient? Why must billions of us go through this elaborate charade of spiritual growth? And why would an infinitely powerful and perfect God need to experience anything? I find this explanation unsatisfying for now, although once we transition we may learn some further details that will make it make more sense.
2. **We are rectifying a dumb mistake.** This idea comes from *A Course in Miracles*, which is a beautiful and wonderfully effective but very complex set of teachings that were channeled to us in the nineteen-sixties by a team that reportedly Jesus led. As we know, Source energy is infinitely powerful and infinitely

creative consciousness. The idea is that at some point an aspect of God had a random thought of the possibility of separation. And, WHOOSH!! That aspect of God was separated. Immediately, of course, the separation was ended. The whole idea had been stupid to begin with! But since what separated was an aspect of consciousness, also infinitely creative and powerful, in that micro-instant of separation the notions of time and space were created. And within separated time and space, consciousness created this physical universe and all the astral realities. Each of us is a part of that bit of briefly separated consciousness, so even though we have been back in God since the beginning of time (literally), we believe that we still are out here and separated, not only from God but also from one another. This explanation doesn't feel right, either, but so far it is the best that I have seen.

At this point, why should the reason matter? We are told repeatedly by the dead, and told by Jesus as a living witness, that we are on earth to grow spiritually, and that the consequences of our not growing spiritually can be severe. We are told that consciousness energy on earth has become so steeped in negativity as a result of humankind's fear-based choices that unless a sufficient number of us can manage to raise our own vibrations, and thereby raise the consciousness vibrations of all of humankind, what we face will be a couple of centuries of rapid and painful decline into barbarism. Even the end of the world is going to seem by then to be a relative blessing.

Seek Your Genuine Treasure

As Jesus tells us, spiritual growth is the only thing that matters. And either we will make progress now, or we risk losing whatever growth we might have attained in all our previous lifetimes. It's important to understand that this risk is real! Jesus isn't threatening us here. He simply is stating a fact that is based in what we might see as consciousness energy and the physics that governs the greater reality. Either we progress or we regress, but we cannot stand still.

"For nothing is hidden that will not become evident, nor anything secret that will not be known and come to light. So take care how you listen; for whoever has, to him more shall be given; and whoever does not have, even what he thinks he has shall be taken away from him" (LK 8:17–18).

Here is a point worth emphasizing. We came here to grow spiritually, but since we have not understood that fact, many of us have spent our lives seeking earthly wealth and power. The dead tell us that wealth and power are the toughest machines in this spiritual gym, the greatest challenges we can attempt, and the easiest ways to set ourselves back spiritually. Take my beloved primary spirit guide as an example. He planned into what should have been his last earth-lifetime the extra challenges of wealth and power with which to accomplish ambitious tasks that included ending American slavery in the eighteenth century. Not only did he find some of his goals for others to be impossible to achieve, but his power and wealth set him back so much spiritually that he had to take an extra earth-lifetime as just a regular guy in Wales in order to make up the spiritual ground that he had lost. Please don't make his mistake! Instead, be grateful for food in your belly and a roof above your head, and begin now to give your full attention to building for yourself the only wealth and power that will be yours to keep. As Jesus says, **"where your treasure is, there your heart will be also"** (MT 6:19–21).

In this vein, you might spare some pity for the billionaires now trying desperately to prolong their present earth-lives. Some are so attached to their baubles that they are funding research into finding ways to keep their awareness going forever inside machines!

The truth is that our lives on earth are brief, trivial, and full of pain. That is by design. Nothing of this world that we think we are gaining turns out to be of any value, and attaching undue importance to even modest riches and status can set us far back spiritually. Once you have internalized the simple lessons in the second half of this book, you will be so rich in love and joy and the peace that passes all understanding that you will at last see earthly wealth as the miserable distraction that it always was. **We have ourselves and all the world to save! And the hour is late, so let us begin.**

Spiritual Growth Made Simple

Chapter Five
It is up to You and Me to Transform the World

"You cannot teach a man anything; you can only help him find it within himself."

—Galileo Galilei,
Italian philosopher (1564–1642)

"Minds are like parachutes. They only function when they are opened."

—Lord Thomas Dewar,
Scottish whiskey baron (1864–1930)

"Science is the belief in the ignorance of the experts."

—Richard Feynman,
theoretical physicist (1918–1988)

"In a time of universal deceit, telling the truth is a revolutionary act."

—George Orwell, English novelist (1903–1950)

"The journey to God is merely the reawakening of the knowledge of where you are always, and what you are forever. It is a journey without distance to a goal that has never changed."

—*A Course in Miracles* (T.8.VI.9. 6–7)

It is difficult to look at the world we've made and not feel some despair. The twentieth century may have been the bloodiest in history, with 38 million people dying in World War I, 60 million more in World War II, 1.6 million in the Korean conflict, and another 1.3 million in America's misguided foray into Vietnam. A hundred million people were killed as a result of these four wars alone! And here we are talking about just the dead. Many times as many of those who were alive at the time of each of these wars were wounded or imprisoned in camps or otherwise traumatized, bereaved and uprooted, so their lives thereafter were much impaired. It is not unreasonable to estimate that more than half a billion people had their lives in the twentieth century severely impacted by the tragedy of war.

Civilization is No Longer "Civilized"

This new century is starting out with even worse potential than did the one before it. From turmoil in the Middle East to North Korea's nuclear threats and Russia's and China's increased belligerence right down through terrorism, deadly diseases, and economic turmoil that might trigger conflict, things on earth are looking so shaky that we have no reason to expect this century not to be even worse than the last.

Perhaps worst of all is the terrible fact that our lives are permeated by cruelty and violence. This is new. A hundred years ago the Great War raged, but even in the midst of it our public entertainments were lovely music and graceful movies and spectator sports that seem absurdly tame by modern standards. It was conceivable a hundred years ago to imagine that our civilization was advancing. But after that the lights went out.

It is difficult for people living today to comprehend how deep we've sunk into depravity. Just as fish born into polluted water cannot imagine any shade but brown, so we who were born into the world that was made by the violent twentieth century think our present reality must be normal. Surely modern people are no crueler than were, say, the ancient Romans. They enjoyed watching lions hunt Christians, right? What could be any worse than that?

Our civilization may be no more horrendous than the most depraved in history, but in grim ways it is no better. Violence permeates our lives, to the point where those who want to improve society think that violence is the way to do it. People love movies replete with gore, and our children play videogames so depraved that the words "kill" and "die" trip off their tongues. A few nights ago, I told my visiting granddaughter, a beautiful and winsome child of six, that it was time for bed so she should turn off her iPad. She told me she was about to die, and she would turn it off as soon as that happened.

It is easy now to see how Christians can feel justified in calling us "fallen," and how atheists can assume that no God worth the name can exist if we are made in his image.

Understanding How We Can Repair What is Broken

Researchers in the field of afterlife studies can now demonstrate the following facts, each of which is crucial to our understanding of what has gone wrong with modern life, and how we might begin to fix it:

- **The only thing that exists is Mind. And all of our minds are part of Mind.** This fact was discovered scientifically by physicist Max Planck a century ago, and by now it is well supported by evidence. Far from being just a product of our brains, the energy-like potentiality that we think of as human consciousness is the only thing that is real.
- **Mind is highly emotional.** The irony, of course, is that materialist scientists consider consciousness to be produced by the brain, and they see emotions as nothing more than ephemeral artifacts of consciousness. They have reality backwards! Actually, emotions are apparently primary, and they seem to act as a kind of governor of the consciousness energy that is all that exists. We experience our own minds as emotion-based awareness. From this fact, and from other insights, open-minded researchers have come to conclude that the consciousness energy that brings forth everything that we experience as real is in fact based in what we experience as emotion.
- **Consciousness energy exists as a range of vibrations, of which the highest is love.** In its pure state, Mind is infinite love, and its vibratory rate gradually slows as we move down its range from there. In its most debased state, consciousness energy expresses as what we experience as fear.
- **Our free will allows us to choose to be either loving or fearful.** That is an oversimplification, but not by much! What you see around you is a civilization that is grounded in fear and full of fear's byproducts: greed,

anger, hatred, and grief. A love-based civilization would be its opposite, nothing but gentleness and kindness, where conflict of any kind would be impossible.

Can it be so simple? Oh, indeed it can! Once we sufficiently elevate the vibratory level of consciousness on earth, all humanity will live lives based in love as we continue to experience just a bit of free-will-based negativity in order to speed our spiritual growth. This is why those on the highest levels of the astral places where the dead reside have been working so hard for at least a century to raise the level of consciousness on this planet. They are working through us to save the world from destruction at the hands of its inhabitants.

Of course, you and I are not at risk. If the earth blows up, we'll be happily alive forever in the afterlife levels. But the destruction of this planet would be such a loss to the process of human spiritual growth that those who are trying to save it now seem to be pulling out all the stops.

Raising the vibrational level of the consciousness of everyone on the face of the earth is the only way that we can save our planet from destruction, and save humankind from extinction. That might sound like a daunting task, but because all our minds are part of one Mind—so all of us are effectively one being—if even as few as ten percent of us will elevate our own level of consciousness now, we will be raising every human being's level of consciousness together with our own. We will begin a benevolent cycle that will end with the establishment on earth of what Jesus called the Kingdom of God, where the energy of perfect love is so strong that at last we will have put into practice the second line of the Lord's

Prayer: **"Thy kingdom come, thy will be done, on earth as it is in heaven"** (MT 6:10).

As I have begun to talk about the need for us to work to raise our own level of consciousness, people in various audiences have sputtered, "But what about North Korea?" "What about ISIS?"

I have told them what is the most important fact that you can take away from this chapter. Once you and I raise our consciousness vibrations, even the most evil people on the face of the earth will also find their own consciousness elevating, although they may have no idea why. When enough of us have sufficiently raised our own spiritual vibratory rates, we will have effected the transformation for us all. Fear and suffering on earth will be no more.

You and I have the power to save the world! And because of the way consciousness energy works, effecting this transformation within ourselves seems to be the only way that we even *can* save the world. As you will see if you think about the way that a consciousness-based physics seems to work, anything else that we might try in an attempt to save the earth from human-caused destruction—whether stricter laws, more draconian governments, "righteous wars," or anything at all— is bound to further raise the level of fear and anger in many people. So taking any of those steps would actually make even worse the polluting effects of negative consciousness energy! **The only way to reverse humankind's rapid slide into barbarism is to begin to raise the spiritual vibration in as many human hearts as we can.**

Since doing what it will take for you to help all of humankind to get this done is easy, it will make you happy and much improve your post-death life, and it is the very reason why you were born, you might think of the saving of the planet from destruction as just an added plus. But for whatever reason you choose to begin it, your giving a try to the teachings shared in the balance of this book is the single greatest thing you can do for yourself, and also for everyone else.

Beginning to Apply the Gospel Teachings

While successfully applying these teachings doesn't seem to require specific preparation, here are some things you might do at the start that can help to make this process easier:

- **Try not to tell people what you are doing.** Give yourself the gift of low expectations! Even if someone mentions having noticed a change in you, simply smile. No explanation is needed.
- **Simplify your emotional life as much as you can.** Some extended families are battlegrounds. If yours is one of those, then give yourself a brief separation from family events that might involve confrontations. The same goes for friends and co-workers. Give yourself a holiday from rocky relationships for at least three months. Six would be better.
- **Temporarily pause your other spiritual practices.** The sole exception here is meditation, which can be of help in quieting your mind. But some spiritual paths are complicated, and they involve things like gurus and yogis and altered states of consciousness. Please pause all of that! The teachings that follow are laughably

simple. No other practices are likely to help you in applying these teachings to your life, and indeed they could be disabling distractions.

- **Consider pausing your practice of a religion.** To the extent that your religion is based in fear, it is fostering the literal opposite of the elevation of your consciousness. I have loved Christianity since I was a child. I miss it more than I can say, but in the end I had to stop attending church. I found that just being inside a sanctuary brought back all my old terror of a God so judgmental that he sent his own Son to be sacrificed to himself so he could forgive me for being human. Whatever your religion might be, for you to pause your belief in a humanlike God and open yourself to the fact that God is perfect eternal love will be essential to your spiritual growth.

- **Learning the truth about death and the afterlife might make this process easier for you.** Because fear is the opposite of love, it can help a lot for you to banish the primal fear of your own extinction. I'm not sure how important learning the truth about death will be to your spiritual growth, but since that growth will be easier for you if you can lessen the worst of your fears, it makes sense for you to begin this process by doing enough reading of afterlife literature that you are beginning to achieving the ultimate assurance that you never will die.

Try just to let the process happen, without watching for changes in yourself. When I tried this, I expected nothing so I

It is up to You and Me to Transform the World 47

wasn't watching very closely. What I found was that applying the teachings was an adventure when I had no expectations, and keeping an open and accepting mind is likely to work best for you as well. Let yourself notice differences as they occur, but don't get up each day looking for them. Take joy in the simple fact that whatever might be happening for you, and however it might begin to happen, you are doing the best that you can do to foster your own eternal wellbeing and that of the entire world.

As I was doing this program, I found little tricks that made the process feel more efficient. I'll share with you in the chapters that follow the practices that worked best for me, but your process of growth will be unique to you. Perhaps you will find other tricks that work better. If you discover additional techniques that you believe are especially effective for you, please share them with me through *robertagrimes.com* and I'll be happy to pass your ideas on to others who also are undertaking this journey. Let's help one another to help the world!

The following three chapters can be your key to spiritual growth and personal joy, and to a glorious future for this treasured planet. The Gospel steps toward spiritual growth turn out to be an integrated system, a process, and they must be taken in order if they are to transform us internally. There is nothing wrong with applying all three at once, if that is comfortable for you. Only know that until you are living in gratitude, universal forgiveness will be harder for you; and until your forgiveness is so automatic that you never even find resentments rising, achieving the perfect love that is the highest level of human consciousness is going to be sadly impossible for you. **I wish you delight in your fulfilling at last the purpose for which you were born! I am thrilled to contemplate the fact that you are about to enter a joy and a peace and an utter freedom from fear that can suffuse your future life with bliss.**

Chapter Six
An Attitude of Gratitude

"It is through gratitude for the present moment that the spiritual dimension of life opens up."

—Eckhart Tolle,
German-Canadian spiritual philosopher

"Gratitude bestows reverence, allowing us to encounter everyday epiphanies, those transcendent moments of awe that change forever how we experience life and the world."

—John Milton,
English poet and polemicist (1608–1674)

"Gratitude is not only the greatest of virtues, but the parent of all the others."

—Marcus Tullius Cicero,
Roman Philosopher (107–43 BC)

"Often people ask how I manage to be happy despite having no arms and no legs. The quick answer is that I have a choice. I can be angry about not having limbs, or I can be thankful that I have a purpose. I chose gratitude."

—Nick Vujicic, motivational speaker

"For me, every hour is grace. And I feel gratitude in my heart each time I can meet someone and look at his or her smile."

—Elie Wiesel, Holocaust survivor, winner of the
1986 Nobel Peace Prize (1928–2016)

Cultivating an attitude of gratitude turns out to be important preparation for our efforts to grow spiritually. To understand why this is true, please remember two points:

- **Your mind is a powerful part of eternal Mind.** At this moment, your powerful mind is creating the fear- and negativity-filled reality that you think you see around you. This is not your fault. You don't know any better! But the river you are swimming in now is a sewer of counterproductive feelings. To begin to clear away all of that is essential if you are ever to create the joy-filled life that is your birthright.
- **Your mind has created in you a core belief in your own negativity.** Primal human fear and all the negative emotions that derive from fear seem to you to be both real and powerful aspects of who you actually are. You have been taught by your religion and by your culture to believe that you are fearful, evil, fallen, and sadly unworthy. Until you can elevate your mind above all these debilitating false beliefs, you cannot raise your consciousness vibration at all.

In other words, you have repair work to do! And cultivating an attitude of gratitude is the most efficient way for you to bring your negatively-programmed mind to a more open position where its positive programming can begin.

Understanding How Genuine Gratitude Works

Here are some points to keep in mind about gratitude as we begin to apply it:

An Attitude of Gratitude

- **Gratitude must be independent of whatever you see as the current facts of your life.** It is an attitude of mind, and because it is that you can be grateful no matter what is going on. If you have trouble doing that—if your emotions remain tied to objects and events—then you will need to put more effort into breaking that false connection between things and your reactions to them so you can begin to cultivate gratitude as your mind's new set-point.
- **Living in gratitude will help to ensure that you spot all the good things in your life.** Watching studiously for reasons to be grateful tends to crowd out negative thoughts and the sorry notion that you are evil, and to replace it all with a focus on your beautiful new life now a-building.
- **Gratitude begins the process of raising your spiritual vibration.** When you are concentrating on negative emotions, you are weighing yourself down with spiritual lead! When your focus shifts toward being grateful, you can begin to jettison that leaden detritus and focus instead on what is good. You will find that beginning to do this feels powerful!
- **Gratitude makes you happier.** This may be true because looking for reasons to be grateful helps you to notice them; or it may be true just because a grateful attitude of mind is in itself a form of happiness. But if you want to be happier, looking at your life with an attitude of gratitude is where happiness begins.

- **Gratitude is a way for you to begin to create your own best life.** Since your mind is continuously creating the reality that you think you see around you, concentrating on reasons for being grateful is a powerful way for you to begin to elevate what your mind is creating. Praying in gratitude affirmations seems almost to guarantee a better outcome.

Your personal gratitude practice is something that you will develop for yourself. What works for you may not work for someone else, but I urge you to try what has worked for others before you settle on what will be your own best practice forevermore. Here are four options that have been shown to work well for many people:

1. **Keep a gratitude journal.** Some people make a point of noticing and writing down at least one new thing every day that they are grateful for, then also writing down why they are grateful for it. This can be easy for perhaps the first month, but after you have journaled the obvious things and gotten down to journaling the subtle things like air and sunshine, and then after that you have searched for reasons to be grateful even for garbage and mosquitoes and air pollution and the neighbor's dog barking in the night, you will find that journaling forces you to go ever deeper into what gratitude even means.
2. **Share your attitude of gratitude with others.** In a society that seems to be focused on downers, it is time for you to eschew the espousal of even the most obvious negative thoughts. Instead, you might say of

a hated politician, "I'm grateful for the fact that he's a really good father. Have you noticed how well his children turned out?" Or you might say of your city's twentieth straight day of rain, "The news says the reservoirs are filling up. I'm so grateful for that! Aren't you?" Or if everyone is cranky about working extra hours so you can meet a deadline, you'll say, "I'm so grateful for that shop on the corner that's open 'til midnight. We can get sandwiches!" Or perhaps, "Do you know what this project makes me grateful for? I'm getting to know you all so much better." Not only will your habit of always speaking from an attitude of gratitude reinforce your personal gratitude practice, but it will help those with whom you share these thoughts to begin to cultivate gratitude in themselves.

3. **Let gratitude replace your every resentment.** Resentments will continue to rise in you until you have perfected your forgiveness practice, but your work on gratitude will help you to recognize them promptly and begin to deal with them. Whenever you suffer cranky thoughts about some relative who is refusing to get a clue, or some problem that is plaguing your car's engine when you can't spare the funds to get it fixed, or really anything at all that seems to be a current downer in your life, look immediately for something wonderful about that person or thing for which you can feel gratitude. You needn't write it down or even say it aloud, but at least make sure that you clearly form a thought about what you have found to be grateful for in your awful relative or your failing engine. Let your

gratitude swell and smother your irritation. You will see in the next chapter how much your having cultivated this practice as a first step will help when you turn your emphasis toward establishing your habit of prevenient forgiveness.

4. **Pray only in gratitude affirmations.** Never again in your life pray from lack! When you say, "Dear God, please fix this," you are affirming with your mind the brokenness of whatever you want to see mended, and that in turn makes the improvement more difficult. Instead of claiming the lack, claim the gift. And when you say "Thank you" for whatever gift or cure your affirmation prayer is claiming, you seem to be turbo-charging your request. This glorious twilight of my life when I live in the perfect joy of service began when I started to pray, **"Thank You for giving me work to do. Thank You for showing me how to do it,"** and thereby gave my life to God. It was that simple! I pray those affirmations to this day, and the pleasures that flow from my impulsive gift are beyond my ability to express them.

My suggestion is that you apply all four of these gratitude practices right now, and thereby begin to prepare your mind for more rapid spiritual growth to come. You might choose not to continue to journal beyond the first month or two, which is fine. But for you to continue the remaining three gratitude practices for the rest of your life will be the equivalent of forever maintaining your grounding in ever greater spiritual health.

The extent to which you will need to actively practice gratitude will depend upon how naturally it comes to you.

An Attitude of Gratitude

Many people take to it easily as a kind of cheerful game, and it may be only weeks before you are glad to feel grateful for just about everything. It will be time then—or whenever you feel ready—to turn your mind with confidence toward the single most crucial skill that you can master in this tough game of life. **Let's talk now about forgiveness. This is not for sissies!**

Chapter Seven
Universal Forgiveness

"Do not judge so that you will not be judged. For in the way you judge, you will be judged; and by your standard of measure, it will be measured to you."

— Jesus (MT 7:1–2)

"But I say to you, do not resist an evil person; but whoever slaps you on your right cheek, turn the other to him also. If anyone wants to sue you and take your shirt, let him have your coat also. Whoever forces you to go one mile, go with him two."

— Jesus (MT 5:39–41)

"If someone succeeds in provoking you, realize that your mind is complicit in the provocation."

— Epictetus, Stoic philosopher (55–135)

"The weak can never forgive. Forgiveness is the attribute of the strong."

— Mahatma Gandhi,
Indian leader and mystic (1869–1948)

"Forgiveness is not an occasional act, it is a constant attitude."

— Martin Luther King, Jr.,
winner of the 1964 Nobel Peace Prize (1929–1968)

"He who is devoid of the power to forgive is devoid of the power to love."

— Martin Luther King, Jr.,
winner of the 1964 Nobel Peace Prize (1929–1968)

Of the two core spiritual practices that Jesus teaches in the Gospels, forgiveness is the one that we have trouble learning. Yet learning how to perfectly forgive must come before we can really learn how to love! It is not an exaggeration to say that until you have mastered universal forgiveness – or what we might more precisely call prevenient forgiveness – you won't be able even to fathom what it means to love as Jesus taught us to love, in a manner that actually transforms us internally. But lesser kinds of love come naturally. Love is emotion at its highest vibration, so even a temporary taste of it feels so delicious that we spend our lives seeking moments of love as if it were a drug. On the other hand, forgiveness feels like a difficult and unnatural response to unpleasant emotions that lie at the bottom of the consciousness vibratory scale. The tedious process of forgiveness can make us feel even worse than we already feel about whatever it is that we are trying to forgive. No wonder we would rather not do it!

Failure to Forgive Will Block Your Spiritual Growth

For reasons that will soon become clear, learning to forgive immediately and completely is a necessary precursor to our making spiritual progress. I have come to think that unless we have developed a habit of automatic prevenient forgiveness, we cannot love even family members and treasured soul mates with any consistency. Forgiveness is the seed that we plant in earth that gratitude has tilled, and from it springs the abundant love that is the essence and the goal of our spiritual growth.

Sadly, modern religions discount the importance of forgiveness, and modern secular cultures ignore it, which seems to be a major reason why humankind remains so spiritually bankrupt. Let's look at some facts about forgiveness, and then let's explore a technique that can make what seems to be impossible actually pretty simple:

- **Forgiveness applies to situations as well as to people.** Forgiveness is the appropriate response to every low-vibration emotion, from anger and resentment through fear and grief. Harboring any low-vibration emotion will kill your ability to grow spiritually, so it is these negative emotions that are your enemy, not whatever might have given them rise. Anyone or anything that triggers your resentment is your call to immediate and complete forgiveness, from a long flight delay to your loss of a job to your mother-in-law's irritating boyfriend. If it raises your ire, then you have to forgive it at once or your spiritual train is derailed.
- **Forgiveness is the gift that you give to yourself.** Your mother-in-law's boyfriend and the flight delay could not care less whether you forgive them, but you care very much about the fact that your irritation about them has ruined your day! It isn't even necessary to tell them you are forgiving them, unless that seems to be important to you. Forgiveness is for yourself! It is *always* for yourself. Perhaps your keeping this fact in mind will make your learning process easier.
- **Forgiveness is not approval.** If someone harms you or harms someone you love, or even if you learn about

someone who has notoriously harmed a stranger, immediate and complete forgiveness is essential. But you needn't—and you likely shouldn't— attempt to approve of whatever has been done.

- **You don't have to keep the offender in your life.** In family situations, it may be important that you forgive and then work to rebuild the relationship; but otherwise, it is fine if you simply forgive and release the offender with your love. And if a relationship is abusive or damaging, you can forgive and then separate yourself altogether.
- **There is no wrong that cannot be forgiven.** When you treat forgiveness as an exercise that is essential to your own spiritual health, you will find that there is not as much difference as you might imagine between forgiving a stubbed toe and forgiving a murder. Human minds are eternal! When measured against forever, these unpleasant interactions with others on earth really amount to precisely nothing.

Forgiving the Unforgivable

There are people who have read my fifth point above and immediately bristled with outrage. How can I equate a stubbed toe with a murder? I hear from folks whose soul-mates have died, or whose children's lives have been taken by others, and for whom the unfairness of their personal tragedies has become the brooding center of their lives. I understand that for me to say that recovering from this deep-seated pain is even possible might feel to them like a personal attack. I get that. And if protecting your right to nurture your anger and grief still seems essential to you, then of course your life's decisions are your own. But please understand that:

- **Your dead loved ones want you to go on and grow spiritually.** The dead say this universally! Every dead spouse wants the survivor to love again. Every dead child is desperate to reassure grieving parents that he or she is growing up in joy and will be there to greet them at their deathbeds. If you don't believe me, then please find a good medium and ask your own dead loved ones what you can best do to honor them now.
- **Your grief and pain won't harm those you blame for your misery.** If a crime has been committed, then cooperate with the criminal justice process. But never delude yourself into thinking that the grudge you are nursing ever matters at all to those that you blame for having caused you harm.
- **There is no honor in self-righteousness. There is no shame in forgiveness.** No scale exists that you will be unbalancing if you manage to forgive whatever horrendous thing may have happened in your life! This is about you, and about *only* you. It is your right to choose to lay your burden down.
- **Unless you can learn to forgive the unforgivable, you will not be able to grow much spiritually.** I am sorry to say this, but unless you are willing to admit to even the possibility that you might be able to forgive the unforgivable, you may as well stop reading now since nothing else in this book can ever help you. In having

planned into this lifetime your particular lesson in extreme forgiveness, you have given yourself a wonderful opportunity that can help you to grow spiritually by light-years! But an opportunity is an opportunity only if you are willing to open your heart to the possibility that you might avail yourself of it.

- **Forgiveness is a universal process.** As you will see, it applies to everything equally, so in practicing forgiveness you won't have to dwell on your seemingly unforgivable trauma. Instead, just make it a part of your forgiveness practice right from the start. The resulting new freedom is going to astound you!

I hope you can open your heart enough to see that perhaps forgiving even what now seems to be unforgivable might conceivably be possible for you. If you can give yourself that gift, then the process itself can do the rest.

Practicing Bespoke Forgiveness is Too Much Work

The problem most of us have with forgiveness is that we tailor-make our forgiveness practice to suit each separate irritation. I was doing this, too. It was tedious and exhausting! Soon I found myself feeling the need to forgive even my very need to keep forgiving. There were days when I was ticked-off enough at Jesus for insisting that I forgive that I needed to forgive him, too. This process of applying forgiveness only after you are already upset is so difficult that there were days in the beginning when I felt that I was doing little more with my time than tediously practicing forgiveness. First, I had to notice that something or someone was annoying me. Then I had to try to forgive whatever it was as my irritation was further rising. And then I had to grumpily wrestle it all down and squelch it. The whole forgiveness fight was exhausting.

Even worse, I found that doing all that bespoke forgiveness was not lessening my endless need to keep on forgiving. I was spending my time now defensively watching for further irritations, and then I would go through feeling angry as I worked to forgive each separate time. In desperation, I tried another tack.

You will recall that we learned in Chapter Two that our earth-minds are *lazy, adaptable,* and *governed by habits*. I didn't realize it when I began my new, more aggressive stage of practicing forgiveness, but these three fortunate characteristics give us the opportunity to begin to put behind us the need to ever forgive again! When the Apostle Peter asks Jesus, **"Lord, how often shall my brother sin against me and I forgive him? Up to seven times?"** Jesus says to him, **"I do not say to you, up to seven times, but up to seventy times seven"** (MT 18:21–23). That's easy for you to say, Jesus! But can any normal person really do that? Yes. There is a way. And here it is.

Retraining Your Mind for Prevenient Forgiveness

Forgiving each separate offense is too hard! No one can keep that up for long. So the trick to making forgiveness easy is to short-circuit your own negative reactions, to the point where your lazy mind learns not to bother to become upset about anything. **We call it "prevenient forgiveness."** Anticipatory forgivingness. Forgiving everything before it actually happens!

It amounts to retraining your mind to never again be bothered at all, so effectively you have already forgiven every future wrong that ever will happen in your life.

Once you have established your gratitude practice and you are ready to take on forgiveness, too, simply set aside the next few weeks to master forgiveness, once and for all. This takes a little time at the start, so don't attempt it when you are saddled with distractions. You will need to watch for potential irritations before they even have a chance to get started; and then you will have to act right away, before a low-energy emotion can grab mind-space.

Whenever you notice something that you know is going to irritate you, use your hands to gather it all up at once and form it into a nice, tight ball. You can do this in your mind, of course, especially if it happens while driving, but it works best if you will ignore how foolish this makes you feel and simply do it. Use your whole arms to gather every bit of whatever will otherwise upset you, and make a show for yourself of forming the ball. Be sure to include any people who might be involved, especially including yourself. Then vigorously push that ball away with both hands as you say, **"I forgive and I release."** If there are people in your forgiveness ball, say, **"I love you, I bless you, I forgive, and I release."** Say the mantra aloud. And always mean it.

I never dreamed that this would work so well! I began to do it as a short-cut way to manage all those tedious bespoke forgivenesses that were taking up my days. At first, the process of gathering and pushing away might have taken a couple of tries before I had sufficiently vanquished my irritation; but I stuck with it, because within a week or two, I found that doing it just once was enough. And I noticed that my irritations were becoming less frequent. I started to think things were getting better.

Then, perhaps early in the second month of my new forgiveness practice, I noticed that something had occurred in my life that used to drive me up the wall. I cannot recall now what it was, but it was something that happened on the road. I used to be a lethally combative driver, but then one day someone did something stupid and I realized that my need to brake for him was not bothering me at all.

In fact, now nothing was bothering me. Things that used to upset me still were happening, and I still noticed them, but now I felt only peace in their presence. I told someone at the time that almost in a moment I had become internally quiet, still interacting with the world but at a safe remove from it. All those levers on me that people and events used to pull so easily and make me crazy had been disconnected on the inside, somehow. Now people could pull on them all day long! I still felt no emotion but mildness and peace.

When you have been transformed in what seems to be only a moment from someone with a hair-trigger temper to someone who never even feels irritation, that is very big news indeed! I started this exercise with no expectations, so it took me awhile to comprehend the extent to which I had been internally changed.

And this change seems to be permanent. Ever since the end of 2011, I have felt no irritation, no anger, no outrage, no negative emotion beyond a sigh or two when something has gone badly wrong. And no fear! At first, I thought that my new lack of fear was a product of my having finally vanquished humanity's core fear, which is the fear of death; but my lack of fear seems to be just as much the product of this internal softness and peace. The Apostle Paul talks about God's **"peace that passes all understanding"** (Phil 4:7) which fills our hearts and minds. It is only now that I know how that feels. How simple this turns out to be!

Understanding How Prevenient Forgiveness Works

Let's analyze what practicing universal prevenient forgiveness seems to be accomplishing for us:

- **Practicing prevenient forgiveness retrains your mind.** *You* were the one who taught your mind that someone cutting you off in traffic or stealing your wallet was an existential danger in the first place! Now, by giving yourself the conditioning of immediate, forceful action against negative emotions, you seem to be teaching your mind not to bother with emotions that you refuse to court. Your mind finds an easier route forward, and your ongoing insistence on always pushing anger away reinforces your mind's new route until it has made peacefulness its habit. If you let yourself really indulge in anger or crankiness or raging grief, then your mind will give you more of these emotions; but if you refuse to court negativity, your mind turns out to be sufficiently lazy that it will stop reacting once it realizes that reacting will be a waste of its energy. In effect, you really are forgiving every future wrong *before it happens*!

- **Practicing prevenient forgiveness seems to be a powerful antidote to fear.** Fear is the most negative emotion of all, the energetic opposite of love, and what seems to be the case is that when you are squashing various other negative emotions, your mind stops responding with fear as well.

- **Practicing prevenient forgiveness raises your happiness set-point.** Feeling much more peaceful inside, and with negative emotions never troubling you now, you should find that you like being yourself much better than you ever have before.
- **Practicing prevenient forgiveness dramatically improves your interactions with other people.** For most of my life, I had a close friend or two. I didn't even really like people. But once I had mastered prevenient forgiveness, I found that everyone I met was so much nicer! That everyone on earth is more wonderful just because I have learned how to forgive universally is a source of ongoing amazement to me. And I should add that my husband went from being sometimes so unpleasant that I used to think about leaving him, to becoming at once the most kindly, dear, and loving man on the face of the earth. After decades, quite unexpectedly my forgiveness practice has transformed my relationship with him as well.

What if You Have Trouble Forgiving Yourself?

You are likely to find that many of your forgiveness bundles include yourself. You have to admit that your plane was missed in part because of something you did, or that your mother-in-law's boyfriend may have been hurt by something you should not have said. A lot of what raises negative emotions in us is to some extent our own fault. So, jump right into that ball as you're forming it. Pronounce yourself to be also loved and blessed as you forgive and release yourself.

For many of us, just including ourselves in each forgiveness bundle should be sufficient to lighten and soften the way we see ourselves. We should find as we begin to move into the dynamic phase of prevenient forgiveness, during which we seldom find negative emotions even rising in us at all, that we also are happier with ourselves. If this begins to be how you are feeling, then it's fine to go on to the universal love phase of your spiritual growth, while knowing that if you later find complete self-love to be hard to master you may need to do more self-forgiveness work.

But especially if you had hypercritical parents, if you did things in your past that still bother you, if you are steeped in religion-based guilt, or if you just find that faithfully doing your forgiveness practice isn't helping you much, then you might have further self-forgiveness work to do before you can move on.

Here is where counseling might be of help. Self-blame is a poison that can blight you spiritually until you find a way to vanquish it, and the best time in your life to do that is now! Beyond counseling, here are some things you might try:

- **Forgive specific instances in your past.** If you suspect that your self-forgiveness problem might come from a specific past event or two, then make a point of forgiving and releasing each such event, no matter how minor or how far back it was.

- **Forgive your past altogether.** Even a perfect childhood or an early success can distort your image of yourself, especially if it makes your present life feel disappointing. The point is to get your mind to stop dwelling on anything other than its quest for spiritual growth. So, forgive and release even the good things in your past. Forgive and release everything!
- **Forgive God.** Christians worship a humanlike God that can appear to be petty and judgmental, and many Christians respond in kind. We might blame God for anything, from the death of a loved one or the loss of a job to the fact that God has never answered some prayer. The Christian God becomes our scapegoat. Since the genuine God is perfect love, on some level we may be blaming ourselves for thinking of God so negatively, so it makes sense for us to forgive God as an early step in working through our own self-forgiveness.
- **Consider leaving off your religious practice.** The way Christian dogmas can make us feel sinful and unworthy is the opposite of giving us spiritual help. After all, if we are so unworthy of forgiveness that God had to send His Son to die for us, then how can we ever forgive ourselves? No matter how much you might love your religion, and no matter what your religion might be, consider forming every religious belief that is less than perfectly loving into one more forgiveness ball. Make room in your heart for the genuine God.
- **Offer gratitude affirmations for your own perfection.** Once you have done everything else you can think of to ease your sense of self-blame, simply claim the truth of

your own perfection and let the affirmation work its magic. You might pray daily upon rising, **"Thank You for the fact that I am eternally part of Your own perfection," "Thank you for this beautiful day in which I am becoming ever more perfect,"** or some variation of such thoughts. Allow your certainty that you are part of the eternally loving Mind of God to crowd out all remaining doubts.

Begin to Live in Mindfulness

Here are three more tips that I found to be helpful as I was sweeping out and tidying up my mind before I moved on to universal love. I don't know how helpful they will be to you, but they continue to work for me.

- **Be quick to apologize.** One of my first clients when I hung my shingle as a sole-practitioner business attorney was a brilliant salesman. He owned a manufacturer's rep that sold some sort of widget to businesses, and the man himself was so restless that he couldn't sit in a chair for long, so he paced around my office as we talked. I remember little else that happened in the year when I turned thirty-six, but to this day I can recall the moment when he gave me the most important advice of my career. This fellow was pacing in morning sunlight, talking about something else, when he stopped walking and looked at me and said, **"Do you know the two most important words in business? 'I'm sorry.' Apologize whenever you can."** He must have seen confusion in my face, so he added as he resumed his pacing, "Whenever I get a new client, I always pray that something goes wrong. Then

I apologize profusely and rush in and fix it. Now that guy is my client for life." I couldn't see his wisdom at a youthful time when I still was having trouble even seeing myself as a grown-up lawyer. But I see it now! We worry that if we apologize, people will blame us for whatever has gone wrong; but actually, the opposite seems to be true. If you quickly apologize for any glitch that happens anywhere nearby, people empathize with you. They see you as honest and honorable. They even assume that if it really were your fault, you would be making excuses now, so your apology helps to get you off the hook!

- **Thank everyone for everything.** Even if you did ninety percent of the work, always profusely thank whoever might have done the other ten percent. Thank waitresses, someone who holds the door, your parents, your boss, and everyone around you. Keeping your attitude of gratitude always foremost in mind will reinforce that attitude for the rest of your life, and will tend to make this whole process easier.

- **Cultivate your mental peace.** That scientific belief that our minds are merely artifacts of our brains has led many of us to neglect what is our only haven. Beyond protecting your mind from unpleasant world news and violent entertainments, try to build into your life a time each day when you can be alone and at peace in your mind. Some people meditate for a half-hour each day. Others listen to favorite instrumental music for a while between work and dinner. For me, that sacred quiet comes at five o'clock in the morning, when my mind is at its most alert and there is a sense of neither time nor space but my mind can expand to eternity. Try to claim your peacefulness at about the same time every day, and usually half an hour is enough; but give yourself the gift of experiencing your mind not as a tool anymore, but as yourself in close connection with all there is and all there ever will be.

Moving On to Learning Universal Love

Don't hurry through your forgiveness process. Learning to forgive beforehand and universally, for the rest of your life, is the greatest gift you can give to yourself! Especially if you have long been nurturing particular low-vibration emotions, give yourself the grace of constant vigilance until you are able to say that it has been a year since you last had to bundle up anything and bless it and forgive it.

Prevenient forgiveness turns out to be an essential precursor to universal love. We think of loving as easy, don't we? But in fact, the sort of love that comes easily turns out to be nothing like the genuine love that comes with greater spiritual growth. *A Course in Miracles* calls the kind of love that you have for just those closest to you "special loves," and it suggests that such loves are as counterproductive to your spiritual development as are special hates. People who have not developed spiritually will fall into and out of love for trivial reasons, the way middle-schoolers develop crushes, and they often make enemies in just the same way. Their emotions are as unstable as the wind. **But for those who have mastered prevenient forgiveness, the supreme joy of universal love can be little more than a heartbeat away.**

Chapter Eight
Universal Love

"We have before us the glorious opportunity to inject a new dimension of love into the veins of our civilization."

—Martin Luther King, Jr.,
winner of the 1964 Nobel Peace Prize (1929–1968)

"It is love alone that leads to right action. What brings order in the world is to love and let love do what it will."

—J. Krishnamurti,
Indian writer and philosopher (1895–1986)

"God loves each of us as if there were only one of us."

—Saint Augustine of Hippo (354–430)

"A new commandment I give to you, that you love one another, even as I have loved you, that you also love one another."

—Jesus (JN 13:34)

"You have heard that it was said, 'You shall love your neighbor and hate your enemy.' But I say to you, love your enemies and pray for those who persecute you, so that you may be sons of your Father who is in heaven; for He causes His sun to rise on the evil and the good, and sends rain on the righteous and the unrighteous. For if you love those who love you, what reward do you have? Do not even the tax collectors do the same? If you greet only your brothers, what more are you doing than others? Do not even the Gentiles do the same? Therefore you are to be perfect, as your heavenly Father is perfect."

—Jesus (MT 5:43–48)

Icelandic has a hundred words for snow, while in English the word for love covers everything from saintly sacrifice to raunchy sex, a mother's care and your affection for your hamster. Surely each of our many kinds of love deserves its own English word! Especially since all love is not equal. Nearly everything that we think of as love is fickle, inconstant, sometimes painful, and always peripheral to who we are. Only one kind of love has the power to permanently elevate our spiritual vibration, so that is the only kind of love that we will be discussing here. For want of a better way to describe it, we'll call it universal love. Or perhaps ultimate love, if you prefer. It transforms you from within, and it makes you joyous! **But it seems that we only experience anything like this permanent kind of love once we have so well mastered prevenient forgiveness that we never experience low-vibration emotions.**

So you certainly should be aware of the kind of love that is your ultimate goal, and there is no harm in your beginning to work now toward the development of it, but please focus on your forgiveness work first. Once you have put fear and anger behind you, universal love will come to you naturally.

Defining the Universal, Ultimate Love That is Our Source and Our Destination

The Gospel words of Jesus on love and forgiveness were spoken by him in Aramaic, and then they were translated into Greek, after which they survived for nearly two thousand years buried deep in the Christian Bible before they were translated into modern English. It is a wonder that we still have any of the words that Jesus actually spoke! And it would not be surprising to find that we might now need to re-read

Universal Love

the Gospel words of Jesus in light of modern humankind's much deeper understanding of the nature of reality and the nature of God. Indeed, what is most surprising is the fact that the ancient words of Jesus seem to need so little modern reinterpretation.

When someone asked Jesus to name God's greatest commandment, he didn't name any of the Ten Commandments. Jesus knew then, as we are learning now, that no religious law is of any help in transforming us internally, which means that Biblical laws are useless from a spiritual perspective. So Jesus didn't name any Old Testament commandment as the most important "commandment," but instead he named as the greatest commandment what is humankind's ultimate goal; and he further reinforced the importance of this goal by equating his rules on loving with what later would become the whole Christian Old Testament. Here is what Jesus said:

"'You shall love the Lord your God with all your heart, and with all your soul, and with all your mind.' This is the great and foremost commandment. The second is like it, 'You shall love your neighbor as yourself.' On these two commandments depend the whole Law and the Prophets" (MT 22:37–40).

Do you see what Jesus is doing here? He is taking all the Law and the Prophets—the entire Old Testament, including all Ten Commandments—and replacing every bit of it with the beautiful new directive that we must love God and love one another as the ultimate goals of human life. He tells us further that what he came to teach is simply the Golden Rule:

"In everything, therefore, treat people the same way you want them to treat you, for this is the Law and the Prophets" (MT 7:12).

Jesus gave us these directives as "commandments" because he was talking to first-century primitives who could not possibly have understood the genuine truths about God and reality that we are learning only now, two millennia later. These "commandments" were not rules at all! They were instead the only eternal goal of all of humankind, our source as well as our destination. And it turns out that for us to get there can be just an easy and natural walk if we first will do the necessary preparation. **Until you have mastered universal prevenient forgiveness, you will find it almost impossible even to comprehend universal or ultimate love.** On the other hand, once you have made prevenient forgiveness your mental habit, you likely will find that genuine love for everyone you see begins to come to you naturally.

It turns out that feelings of love can be tracked by measuring neurochemical correlates like oxytocin and dopamine. This chemical effect of love is so powerful that it can become the equivalent of a recreational drug, and can lead us to seek the feeling of loving as if that feeling were the whole point. So before we talk about the right kind of love, let's make sure that we no longer venture down any of the blind alleys that humankind has established for itself, where love can be used as an emotional drug.

What Universal Love Is Not

The use of love to produce emotional highs is so seductive that some of its manifestations may not be easy to spot, but here are the ones that seem most obvious. You may be able to point out still more:

- **Sex.** Do I have to say it? The emotions associated with sex are the classic upper and downer of drug use. They have nothing to do with genuine love.
- **Romance.** We know the feeling of being in love with someone as a necessary bridge toward marriage, but that intense high of falling in love cannot be for life, even if we marry happily. And if we never make it to a permanent union, then falling in love has to end in the emotional crash of falling back out of love.
- **Marital love.** The emotions of marriage after the honeymoon phase run a daily gamut of highs and lows. As someone who has been married forever, I don't consider the emotions engendered by a long-term marriage to be especially high-energy; but on the other hand, once we begin to master ultimate love, then marriage can be extraordinary.
- **Parental Love.** There is an intense protective feeling that binds mothers and fathers to their offspring and can inspire parents to defend their children with their lives without a second thought. Mercifully, that feeling begins to wane as our children grow away from us; but then, of course, come the grandchildren. I can testify that the most intense emotional high known to humankind is that of a grandmother with her grandchild in her arms. But, nope, this isn't ultimate love, either.

- **Love for Pets.** There are many people who would say that the greatest love they ever have felt was for a dog or a cat or a rat. This kind of love seems to be related most closely to parental love, but since it often is used as a substitute for loving other human beings it does little to advance our spiritual growth. Indeed, it might even get in the way.
- **Friendship.** Many of us have longtime friends whose lives feel like our personal gift. The love I feel for close friends feels more like the steady high of ultimate love, but it still is too dependent on the people involved. Even the friendship kind of love can end badly.
- *Patriotic Feeling.* Whether we are talking about love for country, love for gender, love for race, or love for groups and organizations, it is all the same. That quicker beating and exultant lift of your heart that you feel at the thought of your tribe is just more of the love-drug. It does nothing to raise your spiritual vibration.

While none of these lesser kinds of love can meaningfully raise us spiritually, they are nonetheless important and useful. Experiencing even transient and imperfect love can help us to know how love feels, and it can open our hearts and prepare us to embrace the perfect love that is who we really are.

Better Understanding Universal or Ultimate Love

Even if you are not a Christian, the easiest way for you to begin to envision spiritually transformative love is to put yourself into the mind of Jesus as he is being crucified. No matter what you think might be the reason why Jesus chose crucifixion,

Universal Love

focus here just on the three different kinds of love that he was probably feeling:

- **His love for humankind was universal.** Modern evidence suggests that what went through the mind of Jesus as he lay down on the cross was that his suffering a public death and then his rising from the dead would be his best way to teach the fact that human life is eternal. On the other hand, many Christians believe that Jesus died for our sins. Either way, we can agree on the fact that as he willingly submitted to crucifixion, his mind was full of nothing but his perfect love for all of humankind.

- **His love for the fools who were hammering the nails filled his heart even as the hammering went on.** He said, **"Father, forgive them; for they do not know what they are doing"** (LK 23:34). When you have achieved Jesus's level of forgiveness and love, then your own thoughts, too, will be filled with warm compassion for those who might be doing you harm. As Jesus says, **"I say to you, love your enemies and pray for those who persecute you, so that you may be sons of your Father who is in heaven"** (MT 5:44).

- **Once on the cross, his concern was for those whose own fear and suffering filled his awareness.** He asked his friend, John, and his grieving mother to love and care for one another, and he was solicitous of the criminals who were being crucified with him. When one of them said to him, **"Jesus, remember me when you come into your kingdom!"** Jesus didn't ask the man what his crime had been, or warn him that he was about to be judged. Instead, he felt only love and compassion as he said, **"Truly I say to you, today you shall be with me in Paradise"** (LK 23:42–43).

What Jesus demonstrates for us here in reverse order are the three stages of growth in genuine love as we experience them. *Universal* love for all of humankind is our ultimate goal; *Forgiving* love is possible once we have mastered universal prevenient forgiveness; and *Human* compassionate love for those who touch our hearts is something that we all experience. Each stage of genuine love seems to include the lesser stages, just as nested Russian dolls will contain smaller dolls, so basic human love seems to lead us to and be subsumed by love based in perfect forgiveness, which in turn leads us to and is enveloped by the universal love that is our goal and our birthright.

Learning to master the kind of love that will permanently raise us spiritually turns out to be a process of remembering who and what we already are. If you will keep in mind the fact that this is what you are doing—you are remembering; you are not learning something new—then the process of achieving ultimate love will make more sense as it happens for you.

Genuine Love for God Must Come First

Until I had achieved a greater understanding, I saw Jesus's call for us to love God first of all as just a throw-away line. Doesn't everyone already love God? Well actually, as it turns out, no. Remember that love is the opposite of fear. Love is the highest vibratory rate of consciousness, while fear is the lowest, so it is impossible for us to love what we fear. There is no way around that fact.

You know what I am about to say next. If attending your church makes you fearful of God, then it is time for you to give yourself a temporary break from church attendance. What finally did it for me was the life-size, full-color plaster Jesus that hung on a cross above my church's altar; but what might do it for you could be a stained-glass window, a fire-and-brimstone preacher, or even just the solemn feel of the sanctuary. If anything about your church inspires fear, then please spend the next few months away from it.

Will God mind if you take a break from church?

According to Jesus, God might prefer it:

"When you pray, you are not to be like the hypocrites; for they love to stand and pray in the synagogues and on the street corners so that they may be seen by men. Truly I say to you, they have their reward in full. But you, when you pray, go into your inner room, close your door and pray to your Father who is in secret, and your Father who sees what is done in secret will reward you" (MT 6:1–6).

Your relationship with God is intensely intimate and based in perfect, absolute love. When you have removed from your life every reason for fear, then open your mind and heart and let God in. What worked best for me was beginning to live with what felt like an open prayer-line, where everything that I said or thought was intentionally being shared with God. When I described what I was doing to people, I likened it to feeling as if the top of my head was open, and everything that I was thinking and feeling was being beamed upward to God. If you are still steeped in Christian guilt, you will be reluctant to open yourself to God to this extent, for fear of God's judgment of your thoughts and actions. And even in the bathroom? In bed? In a bar? Is there no privacy at all?

Actually, there turns out to be no privacy. We might as well accept that now. There is no such thing as a private thought, since your consciousness is part of the Mind of God; and not only God, but also all our dead loved ones can watch us as we go about our days. The dead liken this practice to watching television. They will gather for viewing parties. That is just the way it is.

You cannot love your neighbor as yourself until you have established a relationship with God that is based entirely in love and trust, so be sure to give yourself enough time to do that. Live with an open prayer-line until you no longer feel uneasy about thinking and acting while always knowing that God is watching. Developing an intimate relationship with the genuine God feels like an intensification of your forgiveness practice: it softens you more inside; it makes you more peaceful. Being genuinely close to God makes you remember how you felt in your mother's arms. It makes you feel so completely loved that it was only as I became more relaxed about living my life in God's intimate presence that I first began to realize what joy can be. **You are the best-beloved child of an infinitely powerful and perfectly loving God!** Claim that. Own that. Then look around and realize that you also are seeing God's best-beloved child in every other human being on earth.

Find Your Best Tricks for Learning Universal Love

Those three traits of the part of your mind to which you have access while in a body that helped you to learn universal forgiveness are going to make your learning of universal love almost laughably easy. Your earth-mind is *lazy, adaptable,* and *governed by habits.* And when you use those characteristics of your mind to their most productive effect, you can start to intensify your ability to love even before the foundational miracle of universal forgiveness has fully happened for you. Here are some things you might try that worked well for me:

- **Broaden your love for family members and friends to include others.** This is a trick I learned a decade ago. When one of my grandsons was five, I volunteered in his kindergarten class, and it bothered me that I was seeing a class full of children but only one had a halo around his head. I began to experiment with taking that halo — that love, that specialness — that I always saw around my own grandchild and applying it to each member of the class. I was volunteering only once each week, but I swear that within the month I was entering that classroom and seeing a halo around each child's head! When I interacted with any of them, my heart would flush with grandparental bliss. It was real love, too. Years later, unexpectedly I encountered in a store a boy from that long-ago kindergarten class. He had no idea who I was, and his mother was looking at me funny, but it was all I could do to keep from grabbing him into my arms.

- **Learn to create and use spiritual light.** I don't frankly know if this is real! But because your mind is so powerfully creative, it turns out not to matter much whether there objectively is anything to it. Your mind can make some extraordinary things happen. Many years ago, when I was investigating some of the weirder details of what we were learning from the afterlife evidence, someone taught me that between and just above our eyes is a "third eye" that makes spiritual light. You simply imagine that light is being generated there and flowing out and then doing something, whether filling the room or traveling to fill a loved one's home, or being projected to fill the car of some miscreant on the highway. I know this can work, because I have used it to ease people's personal problems without their being aware of it. I even have found it to be a powerful antidote to feeling road-rage. If the thought appeals to you, then as you are doing your universal forgiveness practice, simply add the sending of a flood of spiritual light to everyone in your forgiveness bundle.
- **Make driving into your primary forgiveness-and-love practice.** I spend a lot of time driving, whether seeing legal clients or giving afterlife talks or chauffeuring my five grandchildren. Long before I even realized that it was impossible to master ultimate love until we had mastered prevenient forgiveness, I was experimenting with ways to practice both forgiveness and love as I was driving. These exercises were so helpful that they deserve their own chapter, as you will see.

Universal Love

Beginning to feel universal, ultimate love seems to come naturally once we have mastered universal forgiveness. I first noticed this effect perhaps a year and a half after I had begun my forgiveness practice. I was forgiving automatically now. Nothing ever inspired in me any negative emotion at all, and in fact I was beginning to find the negative emotions of others hard to comprehend. Even grief. My beloved mother died when I was a year and a half into my forgiveness practice, and my only emotion was joy for her, and delight in all the signs of her survival that she soon was sending along.

It must have been about when my mother died that I finally stopped attending church so I could try for a more intimate relationship with God. I had already greatly improved our relationship by keeping for years an open prayer line and beginning to accept without nervousness the fact that God so thoroughly knew me. Removing those weekly reminders that there might be an angry God to be feared helped a lot! To be frank, I found that once I had learned to love and trust God completely, I seemed to be loving all others automatically. To love God is also to love every human being on the face of the earth, which must be why Jesus puts the love of God first.

Living in Ultimate Love

I understand now that for any of us to look at another human being and not feel love and empathy is as foreign to our essential nature as it would be for us to feel automatic rage. Once we have perfected prevenient forgiveness and we are living in the love of God, it seems that we have then remembered enough of who and what we already are that it becomes impossible for us not to love other people. This new kind of love has peculiar traits. I still am seeking to understand it:

- **Ultimate love is devoid of fear or ego.** I see my family so differently now! I no longer see my children and grandchildren as reflections of me, but I love them exactly as they are. I no longer worry about their futures, but I trust in their eternal perfection and surround them often with love and light. It seems that my love for those closest to me has become more like divine, all-encompassing and all-forgiving love. My perspective has changed.

- **Ultimate love feels as if you love everyone equally.** There are no longer halos around my own family's heads! And I realize as I think about this that I don't seem to love them any less, but rather I love everyone else much more.

- **Ultimate love is not possessive.** Oh my goodness, what a difference this makes! If a friend doesn't contact me for a month or a year, I no longer wonder if I have said something wrong. If someone seems not to want a relationship, my love for that person is not affected. I can bless people and let them go and then accept them back if I see them again; none of it seems to be about me at all. My grandchildren can ignore me as they grow. My children can take gifts and not thank me for them. I travel too much, and not long ago when my husband picked me up at the airport, I looked at him and realized that I was neglecting him. I love him enough that it occurred to me that I wouldn't mind if he found a girlfriend for whenever I am away. I even said that to him. He just looked at me funny.

- **Ultimate love is an ongoing process of ever more wonderful spiritual growth.** It still feels like a journey that offers ever-greater surprises and delights as I explore with the unsuspecting people around me how different it feels to genuinely love them.
- **Until we can practice ultimate love, we remain at odds with who and what we are.** This may be the most important lesson that we learn from following the Gospel teachings. They really are a process, and they work by stripping away what is false in us so we can rediscover what is true. They cleanse and purify and elevate us in ways that I never would have thought I could manage, as plainly fallible and unloving as I have been for nearly all of my life. I began to follow the teachings when I was old. Already, I am born anew!

Ultimate love must be pruned and tended in order for it to continue to grow. What our forgiveness practice does is to reawaken in our minds the tendency to vibrate at ever higher levels which is innate to all of humankind, just as a bubble that is released in water naturally is going to rise. But our transformation is a continuous process. Our minds are not perfected overnight, and the way that we are living our lives can either advance or impede that process. Here are some hints about how you might better tend your own transformation:

- **Keep a supervisory eye on your thoughts.** Don't be obsessive. Let your mind play freely, but be aware that you may occasionally need to step in and squelch some nonsense. For example, if you learn that someone who used to be a nemesis of yours but whom you now have forgiven has suffered some sort of setback, your habit-bound mind might think, "It serves him right!" But it doesn't, of course. Squelch that thought at once, and replace it with genuine love and empathy. For you to court even a single self-satisfied negative thought has the potential to set you back by a lot, so don't do that to yourself. Ever!
- **Keep your forgiveness practice at the ready.** To this day, I maintain a vigilance against the stimuli that used to be my worst irritations. I haven't had to make a forgiveness bundle in years, but I think that is mainly because my lazy mind knows that I remain ready to do so.
- **Protect yourself against pointless stresses.** Not long after I began my experiment in following the teachings of Jesus, I altogether stopped watching television, reading newspapers, and going to the movies. I did this mostly because I was having so much trouble dealing with bespoke forgiveness that I wanted no extra irritants; but what surprised me was that I never missed any of it. Now my rule is that if some event that is beyond my control might potentially disturb my mental peace, I would rather not know about it.

- **Protect yourself against violent entertainments.** Whatever your entertainment bent was before you began to entertainment bent was before you began to effect your transformation, you will be aware now that the emotions you feel while watching murder and mayhem onscreen are going to lower your spiritual vibration. Violent entertainments are vastly unhealthy! As the consciousness of humankind continues to rise, the audience for violence is going to shrink; but meanwhile, protect yourself as much as you can. And this especially applies to violent videogames.
- **Be a passive advertisement for spiritual growth.** I can tell you from personal experience that as you begin to really grow spiritually, you will become so flush with the joy of it that you will want to shout it to the world! But don't do that. Nobody wants the details. Instead, just live your love and peace in a way that might be noticed by others. Simply do what Jesus suggests that we do: **"Let your light shine before men in such a way that they may see your good works, and glorify your Father who is in heaven"** (MT 5:16). If you shine your light purely enough, people will begin to come to you; but until that happens, you will best elevate others by demonstrating in your life what is possible for their own.

My wondering how much more I could have accomplished in my life if I had lived the teachings sooner is not helpful now, so I don't dwell on it. I have known for my whole life what was in the Gospels, so why didn't I try to live them sooner? I didn't because I didn't. It doesn't matter now. Whenever I recall that I could have done more, I turn my mind to thinking about how much more is going to be possible for you! If you are still younger than retirement age, you can do so much more with your own precious life. As Jesus says, **"If you hold to my teaching, you are really my disciples. Then you will know the truth, and the truth will set you free"** (JN 8:31–32). That indeed it does. And this freedom is glorious!

As you will see as you begin your own experiment in living the Gospel teachings, you can use those teachings and just the events of your life to altogether transform yourself spiritually. And there is one daily event that offers such wonderful spiritual help that I have come to suspect that God invented cars specifically to be engines of our spiritual growth! You will not believe how well this works. I don't think I could have made so much progress so fast if I had been doing less driving. **Perhaps you are not such a terrible driver as I have been for most of my life, but still I think you will find the next chapter helpful as you look for additional ways to make more rapid spiritual progress.**

Chapter Nine
Driving is a Wonderful Spiritual Exercise

"Darkness cannot drive out darkness; only light can do that. Hate cannot drive out hate; only love can do that."

—Martin Luther King, Jr.,
winner of the 1964 Nobel Peace Prize (1929–1968)

*"If you hear the song I sing,
You will understand. (Listen!)*

*You hold the key to love and fear
All in your trembling hand.*

*Just one key unlocks them both.
It's there at your command.*

*Come on people now, Smile on your brother!
Everybody get together,
Try to love one another Right now."*

—"Come Together" by The Youngbloods (1967)

"We may have all come on different ships, but we're in the same boat now."

—Martin Luther King, Jr.,
winner of the 1964 Nobel Peace Prize (1929–1968)

"Americans will put up with anything provided it doesn't block traffic."

—Dan Rather, journalist

I used to be a lethally obnoxious driver. My most appalling memory is of something that happened decades ago, and to this day it makes me wince.

I must have been already grumpy when someone cut me off on a highway so sharply that I almost hit him as he dodged past me and down an exit ramp. I was seeing through a red veil of rage as I followed him down that ramp without thinking, then followed him down a road and into a park and on road after road inside that park, my bumper to his bumper, abjectly furious. The park was empty, and at some point I realized that my attempting to provoke his anger might not have been such a great idea. I recall praying through gritted teeth that he would keep driving and not stop, but still I pursued him. I was insane, which was something he may have realized because eventually he drove into the parking lot of a police station. I was relieved to speed away.

That was my worst bout of road rage, but for me driving always was a sport of mingled aggression and indignation. I was able to restrain my negative emotions when I had children in the car; but when I was alone, Katie bar the door! I was trying to drive more peacefully even before I began my experiment in living the Gospel teachings of Jesus, when my need to forgive made peaceful driving imperative. There was no way to bundle up with my hands and push away everything that I needed to forgive while driving, and even having to acknowledge that something had upset me and trying to begin the forgiveness process was too distracting on the road. Worst of all, the negative emotions that always rose in me when I was driving would generally pollute my entire day. So in desperation I rethought my whole driving experience.

Driving is a Wonderful Spiritual Exercise

The trick to making this work is for you to make forgiveness and love the entire purpose of your time behind the wheel. You won't find resentments even rising if you have short-circuited them by giving yourself a different vision of what is going on around you. And there is something about the process of driving and the confines of the car and the regularity of it that makes of driving an easy exercise in learning forgiveness and in learning how to love! Let's call these Roberta's Rules of the Road:

- **Give yourself twenty percent more time than you will need to get to wherever you are going.** Feeling hurried turned out to be part of my problem. Now, whenever I get into a car, I carry a tablet or a book, and I look forward to those few extra minutes of early-arrival solitude.
- **Drive at or below the speed limit.** You can't hold to the posted limit if everyone else is driving above it, but if I'm not seeing a few cars passing me I assume I must be driving too fast. If I need to pass someone—and now that rarely happens—I make sure to get back to the slow lane quickly so as not to block those behind me.
- **Defer to people.** Whenever someone wants to cut ahead of me, I wave him right through. Be my guest! To keep my teeth from gritting at first, I used to imagine there must be a helicopter up there trying to spot the most polite driver, so now I was about to win a million dollars. Fortunately, within days that game no longer was needed.

- **Never use your horn.** I used to honk at everyone! My horn was an instrument of discipline, the voice of God if you made a mistake, and a cranky reminder that I had noticed and frowned upon whatever annoying thing you had done. But for going on five years now, I have scarcely used my horn at all. To honk at someone is inexcusable unless you are actively preventing a tragedy.
- **Make up sympathetic stories about people whose actions otherwise would annoy you.** Someone cuts you off? Wave him on with a smile as you think, "The poor man! His wife is in the hospital! I hope he gets there in time!" The fellow who cuts you off shows you his middle finger? Wave him on with anxiety for his awful situation as you think, "The poor man! He has only one finger! The others must be in a bag on the seat. I hope they can reattach them!" Now, I'll admit that for the first few weeks my doing this sort of thing felt ridiculous. Soon, though, I began to enjoy it. And people nowadays so little expect to be treated with kindness on the road that the looks on some of those faces as I would smile and wave them through could sometimes make my entire day!
- **Fill passing cars with love and spiritual light.** In the beginning I was so nervous about the impending rise of road rage in me that I made simply driving in peaceful traffic an opportunity to give the people around me my love. I would look at the face of someone passing me and love that face, no matter who it was. I would think a special message of love to the driver, and imagine

filling his car with light. I found that doing this a lot at first seemed to reprogram my mind into feeling love for all the drivers around me. It lifted my mood right away.

I do not know the extent to which my treating my time behind the wheel as a way to learn love and forgiveness might have made easier this whole process of working to raise my spiritual vibration, but it helped. **Here is what I believe are the reasons why driving makes such a great spiritual exercise:**

- **Your mind is engaged.** You have to give attention to the process of driving, which turns out to be a help as you try to minimize your reaction to negative distractions. On the other hand, you have limited ways to entertain yourself while you are driving, so you have the time to play mental games. When you choose to play games that reinforce your building habits of forgiveness and love, you make the glorious most of your driving time.
- **Negative things will inevitably happen.** You can sit at your desk for an entire day and never feel the need to forgive, but that won't be the case when you are on the road. You'll have to notice what others do wrong so you can react and protect yourself, and if you have established some pre-set reactions that amount to immediate forgiveness, then each negative thing that happens on the road is just another lesson in forgiveness. It's a plus.

- **When you make driving your special time for peace, you reinforce peace in your mind, even when you are not driving.** The fact that I began these new habits of driving as I was learning prevenient forgiveness, and within days they began to work, makes me wonder now to what extent my using driving this way might also have been a reason why I found learning prevenient forgiveness so easy. I don't know. But, as they say, it can't hurt!

How ever you might do it, this can be the year when you will altogether transform your life. No more seeking. No more fear. No more wondering about meaning and purpose, when every day you can ever more certainly know to your soul that you are living your purpose.

Driving has turned out to be for me this whole transformation in microcosm, from my first struggles as I tried to overcome a really appalling driving career to today, when sliding into my car as I anticipate the joys of my time on the road makes driving sometimes the best part of my day.

Chapter Ten
Your Life and the World
are About to Change

"Some men see things as they are and say, why; I dream things that never were and say, why not."

—Robert F. Kennedy, U.S. Senator (1925–1968)

"We must learn to live together as brothers or perish together as fools."

—Martin Luther King, Jr.,
winner of the 1964 Nobel Peace Prize (1929–1968)

"I refuse to accept the view that mankind is so tragically bound to the starless midnight of racism and war that the bright daybreak of peace and brotherhood can never become a reality . . . I believe that unarmed truth and unconditional love will have the final word."

—Martin Luther King, Jr.,
winner of the 1964 Nobel Peace Prize (1929–1968)

"A man sees in the world what he carries in his heart."

—Johann Wolfgang von Goethe,
German writer and statesman (1749–1832)

"You must be the change you wish to see in the world."

—Mahatma Gandhi,
Indian leader and mystic (1869–1948)

We are told by those that we used to think were dead that the fact that humankind has been so clueless about the purpose of human life has meant that nearly all of us have had to live through many earth-lifetimes. We planned each lifetime for spiritual growth, but then we entered each new lifetime devoid (or nearly devoid) of pre-birth memories. As a result, for millennia we have been so unaware of why we were here that we have made spiritual progress only by inches.

Apparently until about a century ago, the elevated beings who oversee this process were content to wait us out. It was only as the bloody twentieth century unfolded, and as the development of atomic bombs progressed, that our lack of spiritual progress in the face of our technological progress began to raise their alarm. To help you appreciate why they are aroused, let's first look at where they now tell us we are heading.

Confronting Our Disastrous Future

Afterlife researchers have known for a while that the future isn't looking good. Since objective time does not exist beyond this material universe, therapists have experimented with future-life progressions in an effort to heal patients' present-life ills; and they have found that after just a century or two, far fewer people will be incarnating and those who manage to incarnate at all will be living much-reduced lives. We who have known about this problem have assumed that a war must be ahead, or a grave environmental disaster; and we have wondered what might be done to prevent it. In a reality without time, and in a reality that is composed of the consciousness-based energy that we have been discussing throughout this book, it would seem that we should be able to prevent whatever is about to go wrong, if only we could learn what it is. Fortunately, as this planet's elevated guardians have begun to announce that they are taking over, they also have shared what is at stake.

What is coming on earth is a rapid descent into barbarism resulting from the prevalence here of low-vibration consciousness energy. Because we still are clueless about what actually is going on, too many people have for too long exercised their free will while on earth to make choices that were based in fear and in its byproducts, anger and hatred and greed. So the jig is up now. The alarming trends that we see beginning will rapidly accelerate, and in just a little more than a century, those who still are coming to earth will be born into a living hell. Here are a few of the problems that we are told that our grandchildren's great-grandchildren will face:

- **Famine.** Primarily as a result of ecological problems, most food will be manufactured and not naturally grown.
- **Disease.** With most antibiotics rendered ineffective by overuse, deadly diseases will have become rampant.
- **Privation.** With all wealth and power in the hands of a few, nearly everyone will again be living in the poverty and desperation that have prevailed throughout most of human history.

- **Childlessness.** Genetic and other problems will mean that most human reproduction must happen in laboratories. And with people so poor, there will be few children born.
- **War?** We haven't heard whether there will be a war, but we assume that it will also take some kind of war to make things fall apart so quickly.

Whether or not it takes a war to help us get there, the dead tell us that the awful world to come will in only perhaps two hundred years cause people who profess to be Christians to mount a religious war in the name of Jesus. Apparently descendants of those who now expect him to return at any moment will by then have become so tired of waiting that they will start an Armageddon on their own in hopes of forcing the Lord to come back.

I find this almost impossible to believe! **Who ever might be so deluded as to think that the end of the world would be something that we had any right to begin?** And having read this book, you understand that an actual Armageddon would only further debase the consciousness energy of this planet, which is why we can be certain that the dead are right when they insist that it never is going to happen. The book of Revelation was the product of a time of great religious persecution, when a desperate man thought that writing such a parable might induce the Lord to return and save his followers.

But two thousand years ago, God came to earth in the person of Jesus to tell us how to raise our spiritual vibrations sufficiently to commence a heaven on earth. He gave us all the right tools! To save the world, we need only put them to use.

Let me say this more bluntly. *Jesus tells us in the Gospels that fixing the world is going to be up to you and me.*

The dead say now that it is not too late. They tell us that if sufficient people will begin to follow the Gospel teachings, we have the power to raise the consciousness vibration of the earth sufficiently to create what in just two hundred years will be a literal heaven on earth. We can bring about the outcome for which Jesus taught us to pray, **"Thy kingdom come, Thy will be done, on earth as it is in heaven"** (LK 11:2). We have the power to renew the world! But if we hope to get it done, the dead are telling us that we had better start right now.

It lately has occurred to me that the book of Revelation might be recognized by modern Christians as an ancient warning. Those four horsemen of the Apocalypse are mounting up now. They are about to ride out and wreak havoc over all the low-spiritual-energy world unless we, who long ago were told how to bring about a heaven on earth, will begin for Jesus and for all of humankind to create instead that better future.

The Dead are Working Through Many of us to Elevate the Planet's Consciousness

We are told that the process of raising the consciousness vibration of all of humankind began around the start of the twentieth century, and gradually it has gathered momentum. Those of us who know what is going on are seeing rapid progress now, little changes every year in a process so widespread and so profound that to describe it would take a separate book. Eventually that history will be written. Only know for now that this is what is happening.

As I studied the afterlife evidence over decades, I came to wonder why there was so little of it to be found before the late nineteenth century, and why it then became so abundant. By the start of this century, for researchers to figure out in detail what is going on was astonishingly easy. I used to wonder, why now?

Of course, over the past couple of decades we have learned the answer to that question. Those in charge of elevating the consciousness vibrations of all humankind are using our increased interest in the afterlife as a way to begin to enlighten us all.

This is not just a Christian problem. The pollution that is low-energy consciousness is thick now over all the earth! There are reports from people who have learned to astral-travel in other dimensions that when the earth is seen from the non-physical dimensions it is covered in a darkish gunk. All that low-energy filth can actually be seen! And those who are able to astrally time-travel—yes, apparently that is a thing—tell us that a few hundred years from now the earth will again be a bright-blue marble. What we cannot yet know is whether that means that we will by then have elevated the planet's consciousness, or whether we will have rid the earth of its spiritual gunk by driving ourselves to extinction.

You Have the Power to Transform the World

You will find a lot of personal payoff in raising your own consciousness vibration. You can better your life while here, and you can improve your eternal life to come. There are suggestions in the afterlife literature that if we will put our minds to spiritual growth, we have the power to make this earth-lifetime our last one, no matter where we started and no matter how old we are now. We will then have attained the upper fifth level, where we can live forevermore in the perfection of glories that are frankly unimaginable to us now.

Of course, even after you have grown beyond the need to return to this spiritual gym, you always will have the option of returning in order to help humankind. Nearly everyone who reaches the point of being able to resist returning will choose to remain where life is perfect and try to help people on earth from there, but I personally know two people in particular who have returned to live on earth after long absences in order to help with the raising of human consciousness that is underway. I'm sure there must be many more. And wouldn't it be good if you, too, had the power to choose how and where you will be of service? Because, depend upon it, your fate and the fate of the earth will be bound together over these next few very difficult centuries. Since your physical death will end nothing for you, it is time to be thinking very much longer-term!

The only way to save the earth from destruction, and to save humankind from eventual extinction, is for as many of us as possible to raise our spiritual vibratory rates. This need was a lot more casual back when Jesus taught us the process the first time; now, however, the need is dire. What he knew then, and what we are learning now, is that raising our personal vibratory rates is the *only* way that we can together raise the consciousness of the earth enough to end wars and bring about the advent of universal peace and understanding.

We have one route, and the time is short, so we had better take it.

I think that by now you must understand that the Gospel teachings of Jesus have nothing to do with the practice of Christianity, so people not Christians can follow them gladly. But what about Christians? Can they also follow the Gospel teachings without risking their faith? What a foolish question! To ask it is to answer it.

This is not just a Christian problem, but Christians are positioned to take the lead. Jesus told us two thousand years ago that he came to save the world from evil, he told us we must be the ones to do it, and he told us how to get it done. Even today, those who love Jesus can have the joy of being for him the salt of the earth and the light of the world. **"Follow Me, and I will make you fishers of men"** (MT 4:19). He is making that call to us again today. The kingdom of heaven cannot be imposed by God, but it only can rise as each of us works to lift ourselves toward more perfect love. **"The kingdom of heaven is like leaven, which a woman took and hid in three pecks of flour until it was all leavened"** (MT 13:33). The Master is telling us that the hour is late. So let us together open our Gospels and begin now to help him save the world.

Appendices

Appendix I
Brief Suggested Study Guide

You may find this book hard to believe until after you have done some of your own research. Fortunately, afterlife-related evidence is abundant now and widely available; and if you want some personal pointers, the books suggested here are some of my favorites. Everyone who has an obsessive hobby is unable to believe that others don't share it, but you may already have your own hobbies. If you want to cut to the chase, I will first give you eight central resources. Read only these, and then go back to living your life with the glorious understanding that those who have gone ahead are fine, they always are only a thought away, and meanwhile the greatest gift you ever can give to them, and give to yourself, is your own further spiritual growth. Or if you find that you have more time, Appendix II is a more extensive guide where I can welcome you into sharing my passion.

Eight Key Resources

The first book given here summarizes the quantum physics that governs our greater reality in a way that non-scientists can enjoy. The second is an accurate afterlife account that was recently written by an elevated being who teaches the newly-dead how to communicate with those left behind. The third is the venerable classic in this field. And the fourth is reportedly an analysis of the Gospels by the One who truly knows them best. All are brief and easy to understand and a lot of fun to read, so please read them first. And the four books that follow them are the absolutely stunning work of one of the world's leading experts on the greater reality and what actually is going on. If you have the time, please read these eight books, and then go on with my love to enjoy your best and most joyous possible life and afterlife!

- *Quantum Enigma* (2006) - Bruce Rosenblum and Fred Kuttner have so much fun with the physics of consciousness that they have done what I would have thought would be impossible. They have written an enjoyable physics page-turner.
- *Flying High in Spirit - A Young Snowboarder's Account of His Ride Through Heaven* (2015, 2018) – Mikey Morgan with the help of his mother, Carol, has written an extraordinary and easily understood summary of his own afterlife experiences. Mikey is a very high-level being, reportedly now upper sixth level, who had last lived on earth in the 1600s. He wanted to be able to communicate with you and me in modern terms, so he took a twenty-year additional earth-lifetime that ended in 2007. Now he communicates through his mother by pendulum, and he teaches people who are newly arrived in the afterlife how to send their families signs of their survival. Everything he tells us is amply corroborated by other communicators. For someone so spiritually advanced to be communicating with us in the 21st century as a modern American kid makes his book important, and it is a cheerful delight to read!
- *Matthew, Mark, Luke, and John* - The red letters in any modern translation of these four slim books of the

Christian Bible are the only place where the words of Jesus are preserved. Early church councils edited the Gospels, both removing things that Jesus had said and adding bits about church-building, sheep-and-goats, and Apocalyptic warnings that Jesus could not have uttered; but otherwise, the words of Jesus in the Gospels are amply corroborated by what the dead now tell us. Appendix III of The Fun of Dying, The Fun of Staying in Touch, and The Fun of Growing Forever will give you further details about the correspondences between the genuine teachings of Jesus and the modern afterlife evidence.

- *Liberating Jesus* (2015, 2021) - Roberta Grimes received this book during two weeks of time from an entity who reportedly was Jesus. Many of those who have fallen away from strict Christian practice love *Liberating Jesus*; although for devout Christians, what it has to say about the religion can be troubling to read.

Dr. R. Craig Hogan is among the world's leading experts on the greater reality. He has lately produced four books that together provide a college-level course on the afterlife and what actually is going on. These books are so terrific that they ought to be on everyone's reading list!

- *Your Eternal Self: Science Discovers the Afterlife* (2021) - This is the updated and expanded second edition of Dr. Hogan's 2008 breakthrough treatise about what actually is going on. Your mind is not produced by or contained in your brain. And your mind is an individual expression of the Universal Intelligence of which we all are a part —we really are all one Mind!

- *Reasons for What Happens to You in Your Life and Your Afterlife: Revealed by Speakers in the Afterlife* (2021) - Dr. Hogan uses information from residents of the life after this life to help to explain what happens to each of us through all the major stages of life: deciding to enter Earth School; planning the Earth School experience; learning to succeed in Earth School; growing in love, compassion, and understanding; graduating; and living in the life after the Earth School life.
- *There Is Nothing but Mind and Experiences* (2021) - Here Dr. Hogan explains that the Universal Intelligence is the basis of reality, and we are all individual expressions of it. He explains how we know this is true, and what it means for your life.
- *Answers to Life's Enduring Questions: Given by Science Discoveries and Afterlife Revelations* (2021) - This is an easy-to-read summary of the contents of the other three books. It is meant primarily for people who want the information but not the detailed explanations and evidence.

These eight works will give you some of the best current information about what makes eternal life possible, what the afterlife is like, how our loved ones communicate with us, and how to make the most of this lifetime so you can have your best eternal life. Perhaps that will be enough. If it is, just let me add that if you ever have questions, you can contact me at *www.RobertaGrimes.com* and I will do what I can to find your answers.

Appendix II
References List

You may be able to perfectly and joyously inhabit the eternal life that is your birthright only after you have done some of your own research! To aid you in that process, here are more than seventy books on seventeen primary topics that I have found to be useful as we work to better understand what actually is going on.

I.	Things Are Not What They Seem	112
II.	Consciousness as the Source of Reality	114
III.	The Nature of Your Mind	117
IV.	The Post-Death Realities	118
V.	The Design and Functioning of Other Realities	121
VI.	Near-Death Experiences	124
VII.	Deathbed Visions	126
VIII.	Signs and Messages from the Dead	127
IX.	Spiritual and Psychic Mediums	129
X.	Physical and Deep-Trance Mediums	130
XI.	Automatic Writing	133
XII.	Guided or Induced Afterlife Connections	134
XIII.	ITC and EVP	136
XIV.	Group Contacts	137
XV.	Reincarnation	138
XVI.	Spirit Influence and Possession	141
XVII.	Achieving More Rapid Spiritual Growth	141

I. Things Are Not What They Seem

Given the depth and range of the afterlife-related evidence now available, it is a sorry fact that the mainstream scientific community continues to ignore it, and even tries to debunk it. This scientific stonewalling is millennia old, although its more active phase seems to have begun at the start of the twentieth century, just as the pioneering quantum physicists were proving that things are not what they seem. Fortunately, dedicated folks have been studying the evidence on their own, so this lack of curiosity on the part of mainstream scientists is little more than an inconvenience.

- *A Lawyer Presents the Evidence for the Afterlife* (2013) - Victor Zammit and Wendy Zammit have spent decades gathering and presenting afterlife evidence to anyone who will listen. If you are having trouble accepting the fact that there even is an afterlife, here is where you might begin your education.
- *Your Eternal Self: Science Discovers the Afterlife* (2021) - R. Craig Hogan gives us an updated and expanded second edition of his 2008 breakthrough treatise about what actually is going on. Your mind is not produced by or contained in your brain. And your mind is an individual expression of the Universal Intelligence of which we all are a part —we really are all one Mind!
- *Reasons for What Happens to You in Your Life and Your Afterlife: Revealed by Speakers in the Afterlife* (2021) - R. Craig Hogan uses information from residents of the life after this life to help to explain what happens to each of us through the major stages of life: deciding to enter

Earth School; planning the Earth School experience; learning to succeed in Earth School; growing in love, compassion, and understanding; graduating; and living in the life after the Earth School life.

- ***There Is Nothing but Mind and Experiences*** (2021) - R. Craig Hogan here explains that the Universal Intelligence is the basis of reality, and we are all individual expressions of it. He explains how we know that this is true, and what it means for your life on earth.

- ***Answers to Life's Enduring Questions: From Science Discoveries and Afterlife Revelations*** (2021) - R. Craig Hogan here gives us an easy-to-read summary of the contents of his other three books that were issued in 2021. This fourth volume is meant primarily for people who want the perspectives but not the detailed explanations and evidence.

- ***The Biology of Belief*** (2005) - Bruce Lipton is a cell biologist who got off the mainstream science reservation and never looked back. Like Hogan's books, Lipton's is so fundamental that it should be one of the first things you read as you get your feet wet in doing wider research. Lipton also recorded a CD set called The Wisdom of Your Cells that makes a great companion to his book.

- ***Is There Life After Death?*** - Elisabeth Kubler-Ross was a physician who specialized in death and dying, and this CD story of her personal journey – told in her wonderfully-accented voice – is compelling. If you don't make the time to listen to Kubler-Ross, your life will forever be the poorer for it.

- *The Secret Life of Plants* (1972) - Half a century ago, Peter Tompkins and Christopher Bird wrote such an extraordinary book that I am amazed that so few people have heard of it. It is a long book, and not directly on point, but if you have the time, please read it. I read this book when it was first published, and even today I wince a little when I cut a tomato or grate a carrot.

II. Consciousness as the Source of Reality

The conclusion that consciousness is the source of reality will come to you only gradually, as you read more and more death-related evidence and you realize there is no other explanation. If you want to speed up the process, here are ten very different books, four of them by physicists, which should get you there more quickly.

- *Quantum Enigma* (2006) – Bruce Rosenblum and Fred Kuttner are adventurous academic physicists, and here they give us an enjoyable summary of their understanding of the consciousness issue in quantum physics. This book is plainly written and highly accessible for non-physicists, so it gives you a great place to begin your physics studies.
- *The Idea of the World (2019); Why Materialism is Baloney* (2014) – Bernardo Kastrup is a brilliant young Dutch scientist who has written a half-dozen scholarly but very accessible books that point to the non-material nature of reality. Here are the two that are most relevant to our research.

Reference List

- *The Self-Aware Universe* (1995) – Amit Goswami is a physicist who understands many of the implications of quantum theory. His book is a little tough for non-physicists. And because it takes into account only Eastern religious teachings, it can be a struggle for the rest of us to grasp. Still, it is fascinating support for the fundamental truth that Consciousness (or Mind) is all there is.
- *The Physics of Consciousness* (2000) – Evan Harris Walker was another physicist. He is said to have been the founder of the modern science of consciousness research, and although he tries to simplify the physics, his book can be a tough slog in spots. Still, I loved every mind-bending minute of it. Walker died in August of 2006. After more than fifty years apart, he is again with Merilyn, the love of his life, who died when they were both sixteen, and (his dedication says) "without whom there would be nothing."
- *My Big TOE* (2007) – Thomas Campbell is a physicist whose consciousness theory of everything is entirely consistent with what afterlife researchers have learned independently. I first met Dr. Campbell soon after this book was published, and I was astounded to see how close his theory of everything based in traditional physics was to the one that I had developed using the afterlife evidence. What wonderful validation! His book is meant for physicists, so it is another hard slog for laypeople. But it is altogether worth the effort.
- *The Unobstructed Universe* (1940) – Stewart Edward White worked in the 1930s. You will be astonished to

find that more than seventy-five years ago he was writing about consciousness as the source of reality, the indestructibility of consciousness, and so much else! There are few books so basic. You will enjoy both him and his psychic/spirit wife, although you may find this book (if at all) only in an antique paperback.

- *Our Unseen Guest* (1920) – Darby and Joan (pseudonyms) worked with Stephen (also a pseudonym), a soldier killed in World War I, and a century ago they published a seminal account which identifies consciousness as the source of reality. The first half of their book is an insightful study of the problems inherent in communicating through mediums. The second half is the earliest reasonably accurate account of the reality revealed by the afterlife evidence that I have yet found. I feel about this book very much as I felt when I realized how completely modern evidence agrees with the teachings of Jesus in the Gospels: if they got it right so long ago, then Darby and Joan both reinforce and are reinforced by what the evidence now tells us. And when eventually some physicist is acclaimed as the mother of a consciousness theory of everything, she ought at least to acknowledge the fact that plucky young Stephen was there long before.

- *The Conscious Universe* (1997); *Entangled Minds* (2006) – Dean Radin is an academic parapsychologist whose interest lies in the workings of psychic phenomena in a quantum reality. Dubbed by some "the Einstein of consciousness research," he never quite says that everything springs from consciousness. But his books are filled with evidence of the primary role of consciousness, and they are well done and fascinating reading.

III. The Nature of Your Mind

If you have trouble grasping the fact that your brain does not generate your mind, here are some books to help you better understand what and where your mind is, and also how powerful it is. Like it or not, the reality you create is your own!

- *Brain Wars* (2012) - Mario Beauregard is a professor of neurology and radiology who has written an engrossing and highly readable summary of the battle now raging between scientists who are still trying to find a source of the human mind inside the brain, and those who have come to accept the fact that the human mind is separate and pre-existing. If you are having trouble making this important leap of understanding, then Beauregard's book is for you.
- *An End to Upside-Down Thinking – Dispelling the Myth That the Brain Produces Consciousness, and the Implications for Everyday Life* (2018) - Mark Gober has written a smart and highly enjoyable summary of the modern case against scientists' erroneous assumption that the brain generates consciousness.
- *The Holographic Universe* (1991) - Michael Talbot's masterwork remains a classic in this field. Much more evidence has been developed in the decades since this author published and soon thereafter died young, but

his book remains one of the most important resources on this subject.
- ***The Field*** (2001) - Lynne McTaggart is an essential pioneer in this area. This book is indispensable background, and she also recorded two wonderful CD sets called *The Field* and *Living the Field* if you would rather listen than read.
- ***The Power of Eight - Harnessing the Miraculous Energies of a Small Group to Heal Others, Your Life, and the World*** (2017) - Lynne McTaggart's more recent book is a wonderful guide to using the power of our minds in practical ways to improve our lives.
- ***One Mind: How Our Individual Consciousness is Part of a Greater Consciousness and Why it Matters*** (2014) - Larry Dossey, MD is a scientist who follows the lead of physicists Max Planck and Albert Einstein in explaining what underlies reality in simple terms that laypeople can understand. For you to begin to internalize the true nature of your mind and the nature of God will considerably aid your efforts to grow spiritually.
- ***The Divine Matrix*** (2007) - Gregg Braden is another pioneer in helping us to understand where and what our minds really are, and his book is fascinating and highly readable.

IV. The Post-Death Realities

We have nearly two hundred years of abundant and consistent communications from the dead, most of the best of which were received in the late nineteenth and early twentieth centuries.

The fact that there are so many communications, and they have been coming to us for so long, from different parts of the world and in a number of different ways, is not what is most significant. ***What still astounds me is the fact that all these hundreds of communications describe the same complex and wonderful post-death reality!*** In decades of reading afterlife communications, I have never found an outlier. I will here give you some of what afterlife experts consider to be the best summaries, together with two older channeled works that are believed by experts to be genuine.

- *Flying High in Spirit – A Young Snowboarder's Account of His Ride Through Heaven* (2015, 2018) – Mikey Morgan with the help of his mother, Carol, has written an extraordinary and easily understood summary of his own afterlife experiences. Mikey is a very high-level being, reportedly now upper sixth level, who had last lived on earth in the 1600s. He wanted to be able to communicate with you and me in modern terms, so he took a twenty-year additional earth-lifetime that ended in 2007. Now he communicates through his mother by pendulum. Everything he tells us is amply corroborated by other communicators. For someone so spiritually advanced to be communicating with us in the 21st century as a modern American kid makes his book important, and it is a cheerful delight to read!
- *The Afterlife Revealed – What Happens After We Die* (2011) – Michael Tymn is a venerable expert in the field of afterlife communication, and his brief book is a

wonderfully detailed summary of what we learn from studying afterlife communications.

- *The Afterlife Unveiled* (2011) – Stafford Betty is a professor of religion, and a good friend of Michael Tymn's. Their books – both brief and easy to understand – make great companion volumes for people beginning to understand the afterlife realities.

- *The Fun of Dying – Find Out What Really Happens Next!* (2010, 2015, 2021) – Roberta Grimes wrote a brief explanation of the afterlife realities for laypeople. This book is meant specifically for those who need an easy summary of this information because they themselves are sick or because a loved one has just died, but general readers have called it an easy and happy way to begin their afterlife studies.

- *Afterlife Interrupted – Helping Stuck Souls Cross Over* (2018) – Nathan Castle is a Dominican priest who helps people who died in an accident, in battle, or otherwise at a time other than at a planned exit point, and who then were in the grasp of such severe negative emotions that they did not completely transition. Fr. Nathan helps them to complete their journeys home. The process he describes is perfectly consistent with what we know about the afterlife and the greater reality, and this wonderful book breaks some amazing new ground!

- *Life in the World Unseen* (1954) – Robert Hugh Benson was a Catholic priest who discovered after he transitioned that his book, *The Necromancers* (1907), was altogether wrong. So through his friend, Anthony Borgia, he wrote a series of books, of which this is the

first and the best. In fact, many researchers consider this to be the most comprehensive and accessible account of the afterlife ever communicated to us. I urge everyone who has any interest in this field to read it, especially since it is now available for free on the Internet.
- ***Testimony of Light*** (2009) – Frances Banks was an Anglican nun who died in 1965, and whose account of the period soon after her death is full of beautiful and touching stories and gorgeous scenes, all consistent with the rest of the evidence.

V. The Design and Functioning of Other Realities

Our biggest problem in studying the realities that we enter at death is that we must get our information from fallible human beings. Whether they speak from beyond the veil, or, like Bob Monroe, they only visited the extra-material realities and returned, our reporters often know little more than we know, believe it or not. This means that it is important to read many after-death accounts, since the more of them we read, the more we can see that each is giving us a slightly different miniscule glimpse of what is the same gigantic set of after-death realities.
- ***The Place We Call Home – Exploring the Soul's Existence After Death*** (2000) – Robert J. Grant gives a brief and lucid examination of the extra-material realities based primarily on the Edgar Cayce materials. I have concerns about relying on Cayce because some of his predictions have been wrong. (Actually, my studies suggest legitimate reasons for his errors, but a treatise on Cayce is, like so much else, beyond the scope of this

book.) Because Grant's book is simply written, and what he reports is reasonably consistent with other sources, his book may be a good introduction.

- *Journeys Out of the Body* (1971); *Far Journeys* (1985); *Ultimate Journey* (1994) – Robert Monroe was a successful businessman with an interesting hobby. At about age 40, he learned how to leave his physical body whenever he liked and travel in extra-material realities, which afterlife researchers call the astral plane. A bright and ruthlessly honest researcher, he wrote three books that together present a gripping story of his own development. Monroe's books detail these realities from the viewpoint of someone who has not died, and therefore he was not protected in his travels as you and I will be at death. From his out-of-body perspective we see less of the scenery and more of the scaffolding. What is interesting about his books to me is the fact that nevertheless Monroe describes essentially the same beyond-material realities that we discover from other sources. His perspective lets us better appreciate how lovingly the post-death process is designed to protect and nurture our minds.
- *Cosmic Journeys* (1999) – Rosalind A. McKnight was one of Bob Monroe's Explorers, the volunteers who replicated his out-of-body work under laboratory conditions. Her book describes her experiences as a naïve and untrained but fearless participant. The first part is a bit silly, but the second half is great, and the view of astral reality that she sets forth here is amply corroborated elsewhere.

Reference List

- *After We Die, What Then?* (1987); *Enjoy Your Own Funeral* (1999) – George W. Meek spent his retirement studying the after-death realities. His books are easy and enjoyable reads, and they contain useful diagrams of the upper levels and the nesting of your various bodies – so long as you always remember that all the levels and bodies exist in the same place (to the extent that talking about "place" means anything). Meek was an important Instrumental Transcommunication (ITC) and Electronic Voice Phenomena (EVP) pioneer, so his books also contain interesting sections on these topics.
- *Journey of Souls* (1994); *Destiny of Souls* (2000) – Michael Newton hypnotically regressed a number of people in deep trance to what they said were their lives between lives, and he reported in these books what they told him. After having read many tales from dead people, I was astonished to read these books and find that the accounts they contained were different from most of the others. They seemed oddly impersonal, even mechanical, although the after-death process that they described was consistent with what I had found elsewhere. It was only later that I thought about the possibility that when we are under deep hypnosis, we may be accessing our eternal subconscious (or superconscious) minds rather than the conscious minds of the individuals who have just died. If that is true, then these books are interesting for that fact alone. Most of what they say is reasonably consistent with other evidence, although they also contain some things that I have not been able to corroborate. These shouldn't be the

first books on this topic that you read, but later on if you are curious and open-minded, you might enjoy them.
- ***Our Unseen Guest*** (1920); ***The Unobstructed Universe*** (1940) – Darby and Joan and Stewart Edward White were colleagues a century ago, and the two books listed here are the earliest reasonably accurate modern summaries of afterlife details that I have found. The fact that I came across them only after I had pieced together most of this from other sources made them astounding to me, although if I had read them decades ago, I might not have taken them seriously. These books are highly readable, and you will find them to be both informative and still on the cutting edge. I urge you to read them, even though you will find them only in libraries or in used paperbacks.

VI. Near-Death Experiences

We are consistently told by those who are dead that death is always a one-way trip, and people who return from NDEs never actually reach the afterlife levels. This is why many accounts of their experiences are aberrant and tinged with religious symbols meant to comfort them. The primary value to the rest of us of stories told by NDE experiencers is the wonderful sense that most of them have of an all-pervading love, and the plain assurance that people's minds can function independently of their bodies. Since they are coming back, those assisting experiencers through their NDEs and back into their bodies will give them only experiences that will further their earthly spiritual growth, and will work to avoid burdening them with imagery that might confuse or trouble them.

- ***Evidence of the Afterlife*** (2010) - Jeffrey Long, with Paul Perry, has published what is billed as the largest study of near-death experiences ever conducted. It focuses on statistical compilations of many experiences gleaned through his website, and it also shows how common NDE details (like the fact that those blind from birth are able to see during NDEs) help to prove the reality that our minds can function apart from our bodies. Long and Perry claim that their book "reveals proof of life after death." If you need to see such proof before you venture ahead, then their book is for you.
- ***Beyond the Light*** (Revised Edition – 2009) - P.M.H. Atwater had three NDEs in 1977, and she spent the next four decades investigating the phenomenon. NDEs are highly variable from individual to individual, but they are consistent across cultures. The fact that infants and young children have the same experiences that adults do (except that they don't have unpleasant NDEs) helps to prove that NDEs are more than just suggestion-induced fantasies. Atwater has written more than a dozen good books, including the enormous and daunting ***The Big Book of Near-Death Experiences*** (2007), but this one seems to be the best for our purposes.
- ***Life After Life*** (1975); ***The Light Beyond*** (1988) - Raymond A. Moody, Jr., is the first popularizer of near-death experiences, and by now he is something of a legend. The experiences that he describes are commonly reported by people who attend a lot of deaths.
- ***Ordered to Return*** (originally published as ***My Life After Dying***, 1991) - George G. Richie, Jr., had what may be the

most elaborately detailed near-death experience ever, and his brief book is a classic in this field. Moody calls it "the best such book in print."

VII. Deathbed Visions

Less well known today than near-death experiences are deathbed visions, even though they appear to be a universal part of dying. All the books listed here are enjoyable and fascinating, and I suggest that you read at least one of them.

- *Death-Bed Visions* (1926) - Sir William Barrett wrote what remains the classic work on deathbed visions, and his brief book is a wonderful read. Unfortunately, it is long out of print and it may be hard to find. Reading it made me see how sad it is that today most dying people are so well sedated that they (and we) miss some wonderful experiences during the moments that they spend in two realities.
- *At the Hour of Death* (1977) - Karlis Osis and Erlendur Haraldsson detail a study of some 50,000 terminally ill patients observed just before their deaths by a thousand doctors and nurses in the United States and in India. Osis and Haraldsson are able to rule out medical explanations for these patients' before-death visions, and they show us that these experiences are much the same in both cultures.
- *One Last Hug Before I Go* (2000) - Carla Wills-Brandon's summary of modern deathbed visions and other before-death and at-death phenomena is a worthy successor to Sir William's pioneering volume. It was this book that

helped me understand why it is that deathbed visions may be necessary. Those newly freed from their bodies are apparently so clueless and confused that without the guidance of dead loved ones and guides they can easily go off-track.

- *Glimpses of Eternity* (2010) - Raymond A. Moody, Jr. has done it again! Having coined the term "Near-Death Experience," he went on thirty-five years later to coin the term "Shared Deathbed Experience." His research indicates that some of those sitting at the bedsides of the dying will see the visions of loved ones and the next levels of reality that the dying typically see, and some even leave their bodies and join the departing spirit on the first part of its journey. As is true of everything that Raymond Moody and Paul Perry write together, this book is an easy and enjoyable read.
- *In the Light of Death* (2015) - Ineke Koedam is a Dutch researcher whose important book is a powerful contribution to the literature of deathbed experiences.
- *Words at the Threshold* (2017) - Lisa Smartt conducted a broad study of the things that dying people say in the days and weeks before they transition, and the result is a fascinating compilation which includes some phenomena that have not previously been observed.

VIII. Signs and Messages from the Dead

Those living on the afterlife levels are far more aware of us than we are of them, and naturally our grief pains them very much. It seems that millennia ago, dead people learned how to manipulate our reality with their minds so they could send us signs of their survival. By now, it seems to be an almost universal phenomenon that those who transition successfully will pause to send a few comforting post-death signs before they venture forth to enjoy the glorious afterlife realities.

- *Hello from Heaven!* (1995) - Bill Guggenheim and Judy Guggenheim wrote a voluminous book on spontaneous signs received from the dead. Often the closest survivors of those who are recently dead will experience communications of various kinds, and some of them are spectacular! Indeed, it has been estimated that more than half of widows and widowers see a vision of the departed spouse within the first year. The Guggenheims interviewed some 2,000 people and collected and categorized more than 3,300 accounts of their experiences.
- *Messages* (2011) - Bonnie McEneaney lost her husband in the World Trade Center Towers on 9/11. Soon thereafter, she began to receive signs from him, and other survivors heard from their lost loved ones as well. McEneaney collected many of these accounts into a book that also includes premonitions and messages received in other ways. This is a beautiful and moving account of a group of people who left their homes one morning not expecting that they were about to die, and then they were desperate to assure their families that they were still okay.
- *Afterlife Communication* (2014) - Expert presenters at the 38th Annual Conference of The Academy f

or Spiritual and Consciousness Studies assemble chapters on the current state of play concerning sixteen proven methods of afterlife communication and eighty-five accounts of extraordinary communications facilitated by these methods. Despite the bounty of information this book contains, it is an easy and enjoyable read.
- *The Fun of Staying in Touch* (2014, 2016, 2021) - Roberta Grimes presents a simple summary of the types of signs that the dead typically send to us, and also of some of the methods of communication that we can initiate with them.
- *The Survival of the Soul and its Evolution After Death* (1921, 2017) - Pierre Emile Cornillier was a meticulous researcher whose wonderful book containing an amazing three hundred and seventy-odd pages of séances held during the heyday of physical and deep-trance mediumship has recently been republished.

IX. Spiritual and Psychic Mediums

I still have trouble believing in the work of mental mediums. I can't get past the fact that they are mind-reading with dead people! And often the dead people whose minds mediums are reading are their own guides, which guides are in contact with our dead relatives. It all feels too tenuous to me. But that is just me. Gary Schwartz's book has convinced me that my prejudices are wrong, and I have recently come to understand that good spiritual and psychic mediums can be very good indeed.

- *The Afterlife Experiments* (2002) - Gary E. Schwartz of the University of Arizona is one of very few academically trained scientists who are investigating the afterlife evidence in a traditional university setting. Something of a skeptic himself, he uses strict scientific methods to study psychic mediums under laboratory conditions with remarkable success. For this book, he subjected some of the most prominent living mediums to double-blind and triple-blind experiments, and he found in some cases that the odds against chance for the results of their readings were in the multiple millions to one.
- *The Amazing Afterlife of Animals: Messages and Signs from Our Pets on the Other Side* (2017) - Karen A. Anderson has made a specialty of assisting bereaved pet owners by receiving for them messages from their recently departed pets.

X. Physical and Deep-Trance Mediums

The late nineteenth and early twentieth centuries were the heyday of physical and deep-trance mediums. What appears to be needed for talented living psychics to develop these skills is many years of passively sitting in the dark night after night, and in the days before radio there were folks who started with fads like table-tipping and went on to become amazingly good trance mediums. Physical mediums in trance are able to produce extraordinary phenomena and even full materializations, and deep-trance mediums can withdraw from their bodies and let a dead medium (called a control) speak, using the living medium's vocal cords. Recent efforts to resurrect both skills in

Great Britain and in the United States are showing some initial promise, but the journey to full development for a talented trance medium is a long one! Meanwhile, I have given you here a recent encyclopedic compendium; two recent books about physical mediumship; two important books by a current leading afterlife researcher; a fascinating set of early accounts by a different researcher; and also three accounts of the work of an important early-twentieth-century team.

- *Great Moments of Modern Mediumship – Volume I* (2014) - Maxine Meilleur has assembled a breathtakingly complete account of the various kinds of afterlife evidence to be found in the annals of mediumship, from the mid-nineteenth century onward.
- *Unfolding Physical Mediumship: Historical, Philosophical, and Personal Perspectives* (2018) - Susan Barnes has written an excellent and easily read summary of the overall history and the current state of play in physical mediumship.
- *In Pursuit of Physical Mediumship* (2007) - Robin Foy has a long personal history in the field of modern British physical mediumship, notably including his involvement in the Scole Experimental Group. His book is a colorful journey though his personal experiences in the field.
- *The Articulate Dead – They Brought the Spirit World Alive* (2008) - Michael Tymn is a venerable expert in the field of afterlife research. This is his seminal book on the heyday of evidential afterlife communication.

- *Resurrecting Leonora Piper: How Science Discovered the Afterlife* (2013) - Michael Tymn's book about the "white crow," Leonora Piper, is a must-read.
- *Spectral Evidence I & II* (2017 & 2018) - Riley Heagerty has made a career of researching and bringing to light the more obscure aspects of the heyday of spirit communication around the turn of the 20th century. His books are dead-on accurate, and they read like candy.
- *Some New Evidence for Human Survival* (1922); *Life Beyond Death with Evidence* (1928); *In the Dawn Beyond Death* (late 1930s) - Charles Drayton Thomas was a British Methodist minister who worked with a deep-trance medium named Gladys Osborne Leonard and her dead control, Feda. He was a curious and methodical fellow investigating what he saw as a cutting-edge phenomenon that was delivering world-changing information. Reading these books in order gives you a sad sense of what a lost period the whole twentieth century really was. Scientists had spent the latter part of the nineteenth century disparaging and trying to debunk all evidence related to mental telepathy and other psi phenomena. Then the early twentieth century brought a flood of afterlife communications produced through deep-trance mediums, so scientists of the day changed their tack. They began to insist that these were not communications from the dead at all, but the mediums were reading the minds of living relatives. So then some of the teams of dead collaborators who were working with deep-trance mediums set out to prove their existence to scientists by devising clever tests

for themselves which would rule out the possibility of mind-reading. Thomas's 1922 book is less interesting to us than are the other two listed here because most of it is patient documentation of the results of these self-tests by the dead delivered to help scientists overcome their skepticism. The dead passed nearly all their own tests, so by the time of Thomas's 1922 book, mainstream science had changed its course again and was ignoring all phenomena that did not fit with materialism. If you have never heard of Charles Drayton Thomas and his century-old book of proofs that were given by his dead collaborators, you know that even then mainstream science's stonewalling was sadly effective.

XI. Automatic Writing

Some of the most interesting first-person accounts by dead people have been received by means of automatic writing. Someone with mediumistic ability sat with pen in hand or with fingers on the keys, and a dead person with similar abilities then wrote as if those hands were his own. The books listed here are quick and enjoyable reads, and nearly all of what they tell us is amply corroborated elsewhere. If you can accept how they were received, they are a useful introduction to the post-death realities.

- *Life in the World Unseen* (1954); *More About Life in the World Unseen* (1956) – Robert Hugh Benson was a British Catholic priest who died in 1914 and discovered after his death that some of what he had written during his lifetime about the afterlife was wrong. So through his friend, Anthony Borgia, he wrote these corrective manuscripts. I came across his books late in my research, and I found them to be so consistent with what I had already learned from other sources as to be frankly astonishing. No matter where these two volumes came from, they are useful first-person accounts of how the afterlife levels can appear to those who are newly arrived.

- ***The Book of James*** (1974) – William James and Susy Smith wrote an entertaining book that is mostly consistent with the rest of the evidence. William James, the brother of novelist Henry James, was a late-nineteenth-century Harvard professor of psychology and the first president of the American Society for Psychical Research. Susy Smith was a psychic and a prominent researcher during the 1970s, when this book was dictated.
- ***Testimony of Light*** (1969) – Frances Banks and Helen Greaves have given us a fascinating portrayal of Banks's early adjustments to life after death. Banks was an Episcopal nun and a spiritual seeker all her life. So many of the details of her account of what happened to her after her death are so consistent with other evidence that her slim volume is well worth reading.

XII. Guided or Induced Afterlife Connections

The afterlife evidence and insights provided by quantum physics seem more and more to suggest that everything that we consider to be real is happening in what we might begin to think of as a universal Mind of which each of our minds is a part. So it shouldn't be surprising that some of the most promising research into personal contact with the dead involves communications that seem to be happening in our minds, while at the same time they are happening in an external and palpable reality. I cannot explain this promising new field, so I'll let some of its pioneers do that for you.

- *Induced After-Death Communication: A Miraculous Therapy for Grief and Loss* (2014) – Allan L. Botkin, Raymond Moody, and R. Craig Hogan have updated and reissued a remarkable book that Botkin and Hogan first co-authored a decade ago.
- *Guided Afterlife Connections* (2011) – Rochelle Wright and R. Craig Hogan are among the pioneers of an extraordinary set of procedures that enable grieving people to meet with, talk with, laugh with, and even hold hands with and hug their dead loved ones. I have met some of the earliest experiencers and heard directly from them about meetings with the dead that seemed to be almost unbelievable. The proof was in the pudding, though: people who had been distraught with grief told me that their grief had been nearly eliminated altogether in one session. Some of them now enjoy regular visits with a dead husband or child. Amazing.
- *Reunions: Visionary Encounters with Departed Loved Ones* (1994) – Raymond A. Moody, Jr. and Paul Perry describe Moody's extensive work in the 1980s with a psychomanteum patterned on the Oracle of the Dead that was used for 2500 years at Ephyra in ancient Greece. Moody and his clients have had considerable success

with this method of contacting the dead. He continues to offer the use of his psychomanteum to seekers, but he tells us that the process of preparation is extensive and "is not to be taken lightly."

XIII. ITC and EVP

Instrumental Transcommunication (ITC) and Electronic Voice Phenomena (EVP) are in their infancy, but this field of research begins to show such promise that we can now pretty well foresee that within a few decades electronic communication with the dead will likely be common. As is true of so much of what is involved in getting this information to the world, the most important ITC and EVP researchers are teams of dead scientists. The biggest barrier to advancement in this area has long been a deficit of living researchers who could act as these dead scientists' patient and very-long-term laboratory assistants. That problem seems to be ending, however, and the dead now working in this field seem to be feeling a new urgency about making breakthroughs.

- *Miracles in the Storm* (2001); *Spirit Faces* (2006) - Mark Macy has for decades been at the center of ITC and EVP research, and his books are a good introduction to these subjects. The first book listed here details how almost a decade of promising research fell apart in the late 1990s because clashes among some of the living researchers caused their dead collaborators to withdraw. The second book includes a summary of some extra-material details gleaned from Borgia's Life in the World Unseen as well as two similar primary sources.

- ***Electronic Voices*** (2010); ***Glimpses of Another World*** (2021) - Anabela Cardoso is a venerable Portuguese researcher working with an eminent team of the dead. She has achieved some extraordinary results.

XIV. Group Contacts

What is needed for real evidential contact to take place between our level of reality and the levels occupied by the dead is the sincere long-term commitment of living people to the process. The dead know who is genuine and who is not, and sometimes when they find a group that seems to them to be worth the effort, a team of the dead will begin what for them is a difficult process and use their living collaborators as a way to deliver validating evidence. The best ITC and EVP have been produced this way, as have been most other remarkable proofs, like apports (items materializing in air), images produced on film, and even human materializations. I have never heard of a team of dead collaborators who began the process and then tired of it, but living people seldom devote the time and energy required for more than a few years' time; and shockingly, sometimes the mischievous dead will interrupt the most successful group experiments. What happened briefly in the village of Scole in Norfolk, England, in the mid-nineties is an example of the sort of wonderful result that can be obtained by dedicated living researchers who are willing to let their dead collaborators take the lead.

- ***The Scole Report*** (1999) – The most extensive report to date on collaborations with the dead is available as a research paper that was printed in the Proceedings of the

Society for Psychical Research, Volume 58, Part 220, in November of 1999. You can find it in many university libraries, and if you resort to copying it you will want to make color copies of its wonderful illustrations. *The Scole Report* describes a scientific investigation of some extraordinary validations that were visited on The Scole Experimental Group from 1993 through 1998 at Scole in Norfolk, England.

- *The Scole Experiment* (1999) – Grant and Jane Solomon worked with the Scole Experimental Group to summarize the findings detailed in *The Scole Report* for general readers. When you read this book, be aware that the full *Scole Report* is even more wonderful.

XV. Reincarnation

There is so much evidence for reincarnation that clearly something like it happens. It's a difficult process to understand, however, since time is not objectively real, so somehow all our lives on earth are happening at the same time. Accounts from upper-level beings suggest that we think of reincarnation not as a linear process, but more as a vat from which the bucket of each lifetime is dipped and back into which each lifetime is poured. Who knows? If you wonder about reincarnation, here are a few good books on the subject.

- *Reliving Past Lives* (1978) – Helen Wambach's groundbreaking study of mass hypnotic regressions is a brief and fascinating book. She set out to disprove reincarnation by hypnotically regressing thousands of people to lives lived in specific historical periods, expecting to be able to record an inconsistent mess of fantasy and gibberish. What she found instead was a distribution of thousands of memories of past lives that included genders, locations, clothing, utensils, foods, and other small details which so perfectly matched the historical record that to have achieved these results by chance was nearly mathematically impossible.

- *Twenty Cases Suggestive of Reincarnation* (1971); *Unlearned Language* (1984); *Where Reincarnation and Biology Intersect* (1997) – Ian Stevenson was Chairman of the Department of Psychiatry at the University of Virginia, and he was a leading researcher in the field of reincarnation. Stevenson spent a half-century studying cases of young children who remembered recent previous lives that had ended violently, and the result is a spectacular body of work which will be celebrated only when the rest of modern science catches up with it. Stevenson wrote for scientists, so his writing style is dry. But the work that he details in his dozen or more volumes is overwhelming evidence for prompt reincarnation in what appears to be the narrow case of unexpected violent death. These are three of his seminal works.

- *Many Lives, Many Masters* (1988); *Same Soul, Many Bodies* (2004) – Brian Weiss is the foremost popularizer of past-life regression therapy for use in the treatment of medical and psychological problems. An eminent Yale-trained psychiatrist, Weiss accidentally discovered the effect that apparent past lives can have on our present life. Unlike other regression therapists who have made the same discovery, he risked his medical career to get the word out. He has even ventured into the newer field of progression therapy (the investigation of how our future lives might affect the present one), which consciousness theory suggests should be possible, although it is a lot harder for us linear-thinking humans to grasp. The result is two illuminating books that offer a good introduction to the whole topic of reincarnation.

- *Children's Past Lives* (1997); *Return from Heaven* (2001) – Carol Bowman has studied the past-life memories of children, and while most of Stevenson's subjects remembered only their most recent lives, Bowman studied children whose present lives appeared to have been affected by traumas suffered in more distant lifetimes. She also has studied the phenomenon of children quickly reincarnating within the same family, which appears to happen fairly often when infants or toddlers die.

- *Reincarnation – The Missing Link in Christianity* (1997) – Elizabeth Clare Prophet wrote a scholarly but highly readable exposition of reincarnation as an original Christian belief. People who doubt that reincarnation was taught and believed by the earliest Christians owe it to themselves to read this book.

- *Your Soul's Plan* (2009) – Robert Schwartz wrote the definitive work on the fact that nearly all of us write life-plans before our births, and these can contain what we might consider to be negative events. Understanding why sometimes very bad things happen for our own spiritual good can help us to make the most of crucial lessons, and might perhaps reduce the need for us to return for additional lifetimes.

XVI. Spirit Influence and Possession

You may or may not take seriously something for which there is considerable evidence: it seems to be possible for living people to be influenced or even possessed by spirits of the dead. Indeed, the condition may even be common, and it may be the cause of any number of otherwise inexplicable maladies. Who knows? Unlike mediumship and near-death experiences, possession has scarcely been studied at all, and spirit-releasement therapy is seldom practiced now because state regulators and malpractice insurers frown on it. This attitude can be expected to change once eternal Mind is shown to be the source of reality. Meanwhile, those few therapists who have made their careers in spirit-releasement therapy (the process of coaxing possessing beings away from their victims and toward the loved ones waiting for them) have had such apparent success that you may find these books fascinating.

- ***People Who Don't Know They're Dead*** (2005) - Gary Leon Hill wrote a quick and enjoyable book that is a useful introduction to the topic.
- ***Healing Lost Souls*** (2003) - William J. Baldwin was a late-twentieth-century expert in this field.

XVII. Achieving More Rapid Spiritual Growth

There have been a number of good things to come from the nascent science of afterlife studies, even beyond the obvious boon of our knowing at last that our minds really are eternal.

We also have learned from the dead why we even take lifetimes on earth at all: we come here to raise our personal spiritual vibrations away from fear and toward more perfect love, just as Jesus tells us is true in the Gospels. As the truth about reality becomes more widely known, and as our need to achieve rapid spiritual growth becomes foremost in more of the developed world, there will be many new resources to aid us. For now, here are some important books to help you in your quest for spiritual growth.

- *Matthew, Mark, Luke, and John* - The red letters in any modern translation of these four slim books are the only place in the Christian Bible where the words of Jesus are preserved. Early church councils edited the Gospels, both removing things that Jesus had said and adding bits about church-building, sheep-and-goats, and Apocalyptic warnings that Jesus could not have uttered; but otherwise, the words of Jesus in the Gospels are amply corroborated by what the dead now tell us. Appendix III of *The Fun of Dying, The Fun of Staying in Touch,* and *The Fun of Growing Forever* gives you details about the amazing correspondences between the genuine teachings of Jesus and the modern afterlife evidence.
- *Awaken with Gratitude* (2016) - Hillis Pugh is a guru of gratitude. He teaches it, and he can help you understand how to use it to its best effect.
- *Conscious Being* (2015) - TJ Woodward's book rocked my world. Here are the essential Gospel teachings, arrived at from the perspective of Eastern writings! TJ

writes beautifully and very accessibly. If you really cannot stand to think of doing anything related to the Bible, then perhaps his book will be enough for you; although once you have begun to work on forgiveness, I hope you will soon realize that you also need to forgive Christianity.

- *A Course in Miracles* (1992, 2008, 2009) - Helen Schucman with the help of William Thetford received between 1965 and 1972 this set of Text, Workbook for Students, and Manual for Teachers that apparently was channeled by a team that Jesus led. Wherever the *Course* came from, it is a powerful set of lessons in ultimate forgiveness. If you are ready to try for Level Six of the afterlife realities at the end of this lifetime, then doing the *Course* may be your best shot! Beware, though. The *Course* is heavy learning, and it is very hard to manage on your own. Fortunately, there are *A Course in Miracles* study groups in most cities worldwide.
- **Quantum Forgiveness** (2015) - David Hoffmeister is a student of A Course in Miracles who uses movies as modern-day parables to give us another approach to learning forgiveness.
- *Liberating Jesus* (2015, 2021) - Roberta Grimes received this book during two weeks of time from an entity who reportedly was Jesus. Many of those who have fallen away from strict Christian practice love *Liberating Jesus*, although for devout Christians what it has to say about the religion can be troubling to read.

Appendix III
Listening to Jesus

I was a devout Christian for most of my life. For me, the hardest thing to accept about the afterlife evidence was the fact that it so blatantly contradicts most of the tenets of mainstream Christianity. It was only when I reread the Gospel words of Jesus in light of what I had learned from the afterlife evidence that I realized that two thousand years ago, Jesus shared with us truths about God, reality, death, the afterlife, and the meaning and purpose of human life that we could not have confirmed independently until at least the twentieth century. Thanks to modern afterlife communications, now we can prove that Jesus is real! He tells us repeatedly in the Gospels that he came as our teacher. At last, we can begin to see what he meant to teach. **The afterlife evidence indicates that a lot of what mainstream Christianity teaches is based in human ideas.** The dead don't sleep until they hear a final trumpet. Their bodies don't reassemble out of the soil. Being baptized does not matter after death; having taken communion does not matter; and accepting Jesus as our personal savior makes no discernible afterlife difference. Evidence suggests that practicing any religion in life does not matter after death, but what counts for us when we die is our having lived our lives in close accordance with Jesus's Gospel teachings.

Jesus tells us to *"Ask, and it will be given to you; seek, and you will find."* (LK 9:11) So I asked. I urge you to do the same!

And I see this as a matter of some urgency now, since the afterlife realities are as real as this material universe. As good communications are developed between this material level and the higher-frequency levels where most of the dead reside, it will become clear that mainstream Christianity has not been teaching what is factual. If believers turn away from Christianity, we don't want them also turning away from Jesus.

Reading Jesus's Gospel Teachings

Think how extraordinary it is that we have the two-thousand-year-old words of someone who claimed to understand reality, and to know what happens when we die. Now add the fact that most of what Jesus says in the Gospels is consistent with what we can only now deduce from afterlife evidence and cutting-edge science. This gives us some amazing validations of both the teachings of Jesus and the modern evidence! Such an extensive coincidence is so unlikely as to be for practical purposes impossible. Yet if you share my wonder and delight at finding how well the words of Jesus fit the evidence, I have to remind you that the odds are long against our having available to us exactly what he said.

Many Christians consider the entire Christian Bible to be the Inspired Word of God. Having read it through a number of times, I must tell you that I find the Bible to be so internally inconsistent and so full of culturally-biased and even un-Christian advice that it seems presumptuous and insulting to pin it all on God. It seems more accurate to say that the writers whose work was assembled into the Christian Bible may have been inspired by God, but they heard God through the filter of their primitive lives in the ancient world so they could have garbled some of God's message. This would be understandable and forgivable. But the fact that it might have happened means that no serious researcher can use most of the Bible as a resource when trying to understand a factual God.

The red letters of the Gospels are another matter. Thomas Jefferson said that the words of Jesus stand out in the Bible like "diamonds in a dunghill," and when you read the Bible through and reach the Gospels, you can see what he meant. In a recent translation, Jesus sounds like a modern man trying to educate primitives: you see him speaking simply and patiently, saying things over and over to people who seem not really to understand him. You even see his rising frustration, and his repeated efforts to quell that frustration and say things over yet again, more simply. Put aside the fact that Jesus's followers started in his name a prominent and now widely fragmented religion. Just read the words of Jesus without religious bias, and you find yourself sympathizing and liking him as a wonderfully wise and good man you would enjoy having as your friend. Reading his words without religious bias makes you wonder whether things that he said might be found to be factually accurate.

Here is where our problems arise. If we don't want to indulge in the magic-thinking notion that the whole Bible is the Inspired Word of God, then we have to take into account how easily the teachings of Jesus could have been distorted during the past two thousand years:

1. For Jesus to speak against the prevailing religion was a crime punishable by death. He was trying to stay alive long enough to share what he had come to teach, and he managed that feat for more than three years by using

some fascinating tricks. He would tell what sounded like innocent stories, then say, "he who has ears to hear, let him hear" (wink-wink) to urge his followers to look for his deeper messages. He would give people innocuous-sounding bits of information at various spots along the way, knowing that the guards watching him would change, and hoping that his faithful followers would be able to put those bits together.

2. *Those who heard Jesus speak and passed his words along, and those who eventually committed them to writing, seem not to have fully understood what he was saying.* It is possible that they inserted or altered words or passages here and there to better support their own understandings. We would be none the wiser.

3. *Jesus's message could have been altered as it was translated into Greek and then from Greek into English.* Aramaic is so different from Greek that direct translations from Aramaic to English are nearly unrecognizable by people who are used to modern Bible versions. The fact that the Gospel words of Jesus that have been translated twice are even more consistent with modern afterlife evidence is flat-out amazing to me.

4. *We depend on the good will of those who were in control of the written Gospels for two millennia.* Here is where our trust is tested! There is evidence that people eager to support their own religious doctrines edited the Gospels over the years, which means that apparently words were put into or taken out of Jesus's mouth. This, too, makes the close correspondence between the surviving Gospel

words of Jesus and modern afterlife communications a source of wonder and delight for us all.

A few of Jesus's Gospel words are lumps of coal among the diamonds. He talks about a fiery hell; he calls Peter the rock on which he will build his church. These passages are inconsistent with afterlife-related evidence, and also with the rest of Jesus's Gospel teachings, which leads me to believe they are doctrinal edits, most of which likely were added by the First Council of Nicaea in 325. If we ignore these atypical bits, then what we have left in all four Gospels is a message that is stunningly consistent with modern afterlife evidence. The man clearly knew what he was talking about, since his words agree with modern evidence in ways that could not have been known — and, indeed, might not have been liked — by the people who preserved them.

Let us imagine that we are only now finding the Gospel words of Jesus, and we know nothing about the religion that was later established in his name. We can see from afterlife-related evidence that two thousand years ago Jesus was familiar with facts about God, reality, death, the afterlife, and the meaning and purpose of human life that have come to light only recently. If all that we had were his newly found teachings, the afterlife evidence, and the afterlife science, how might we now interpret Jesus's words?

He Taught Us About God

Jesus told us the fundamental fact that God is loving Spirit, and each of us is part of God. This was radical stuff in ancient times, when most people worshiped semi-physical gods who were more like the Old Testament's Jehovah, often vengeful and hard to placate.

"God is spirit, and his worshipers must worship in spirit and in truth." (JN 4:24)

"The kingdom of God is within you." (LK 17:20–21)

"The Spirit gives life; the flesh counts for nothing. The words I have spoken to you are spirit, and they are life." (JN 6:63)

"If you love me, you will obey what I command. And I will ask the Father, and he will give you another Counselor to be with you forever—the Spirit of truth. The world cannot accept him, because it neither sees him nor knows him. But you know him, for he lives with you and will be in you." (JN 14:15–17)

Jesus took the ancient Hebrews' radical concept of a single nonphysical God and transformed it into what modern evidence shows us is universal Spirit (or Mind).

He Taught Us the Importance of Love

Jesus reduced the Old Testament's Ten Commandments to one commandment: that we learn how to love.

"A new command I give you: Love one another. As I have loved you, so you must love one another." (JN 13:34)

"'Love the Lord your God with all your heart and with all your soul and with all your mind.' This is the first and greatest commandment. And the second is like it: 'Love your neighbor as yourself.' All the Law and the Prophets hang on these two commandments." (MT 22:37–40)

"You have heard that it was said, 'Love your neighbor and hate your enemy.' But I tell you: love your enemies and pray for those

who persecute you, that you may be sons of your Father in heaven . . . Be perfect, therefore, as your heavenly Father is perfect." (MT 5:43–48)

He Taught Us the Importance of Forgiveness

When I first realized that God does not judge us, I worried that on this point Jesus might have been mistaken. But then I considered this series of quotations.

"For if you forgive men when they sin against you, your heavenly Father will also forgive you. But if you do not forgive men their sins, your Father will not forgive your sins." (MT 6:14–15)

"Moreover, the Father judges no one, but has entrusted all judgment to the Son, that all may honor the Son just as they honor the Father." (JN 5:21–23)

"You judge by human standards; I pass judgment on no one." (JN 8:15)

"As for the person who hears my words but does not keep them, I do not judge him. For I did not come to judge the world, but to save it." (JN 12:47)

Were these messages inconsistencies? I think not. Instead, I think they were Jesus's efforts (meted out in bits at different times beneath the Temple's radar) to wean his primitive listeners from their old idea of God as judge so they could better comprehend what modern evidence tells us is true: each of us will be our own post-death judge. Jesus's disciple, Peter, asked him, "Lord, how many times shall I forgive my brother when he sins against me? Up to seven times?" Jesus answered, *"I tell you, not seven times, but seventy times seven."* (MT 18:21–23)

He even hinted pretty strongly that each of us will judge ourselves:

"Do not judge, or you too will be judged. For in the same way you judge others, you will be judged, and with the measure you use, it will be measured to you." (MT 7:1–2).

He Taught Us the Need for Humility

Into that ancient class-obsessed world Jesus brought a rude shock for the elite: after we die, our status in life means nothing.

"Many who are first will be last, and the last first." (MK 10:31)

"The greatest among you will be your servant. For whoever exalts himself will be humbled, and whoever humbles himself will be exalted." (MT 23:11–12)

"Whoever welcomes this little child in my name welcomes me, and whoever welcomes me welcomes the one who sent me. For he who is least among you all—he is the greatest." (LK 9:48)

"Let the little children come to me, and do not hinder them, for the kingdom of God belongs to such as these. I tell you the truth, anyone who will not receive the kingdom of God like a little child will never enter it." (MK 10:14–15)

He Taught Us About the Power of Our Minds

Mainstream Christian doctrines ignore something that strikes a modern nonreligious reader: Jesus said a lot about the power of our minds to affect reality.

"Take heart, daughter. Your faith has healed you." (MT 9:22)

(Healing a blind man) *"Do you believe that I am able to do this? …. According to your faith will it be done to you."* (MT 9:28–29)

(When Peter couldn't walk on water) *"You of little faith. Why did you doubt?"* (MT 14:31)

"Who touched me? Someone touched me. I know that power has gone out from me ... Daughter, your faith has healed you. Go in peace." (LK 8:46–48)

"Have faith in God. I tell you the truth, if anyone says to this mountain, 'Go, throw yourself into the sea,' and does not doubt in his heart but believes that what he says will happen, it will be done for him. Therefore I tell you, whatever you ask for in prayer, believe that you have received it, and it will be yours." (MK 11:22–24)

It is difficult for us to appreciate how radical these teachings were in the Judea and Samaria of two thousand years ago. Jesus used the familiar Hebrew concept of faith in God to teach his followers the power of their eternal minds, and to teach them that their minds—like his—were part of one universal Mind.

"When you pray, go into your room, close the door and pray to your Father, who is unseen. Then your Father, who sees what is done in secret, will reward you." (MT 6:6)

"For whatever is hidden is meant to be disclosed, and whatever is concealed is meant to be brought out into the open. If anyone has ears to hear, let him hear." (MK 4:22–23)

He Taught Us About the Afterlife

Some of the messages attributed to Jesus seem inexplicable and even cruel until we compare them with the afterlife evidence. That is when we realize that Jesus was talking not about this life, but about the afterlife. He was right in telling us that spiritual development is our real goal, and right in saying there is no way to shortcut it. He was right, too, in saying that those who don't progress sufficiently may regress and lose whatever progress they have made, and they may even judge and condemn themselves to the dark and smelly lowest afterlife level, which he referred to as the outer darkness.

"For everyone who has will be given more, and he will have an abundance. Whoever does not have, even what he has will be taken from him. And throw that worthless servant outside, into the darkness, where there will be weeping and gnashing of teeth." (MT 29:30)

"For there is nothing hidden that will not be disclosed, and nothing concealed that will not be known or brought out into the open. Therefore consider carefully how you listen. Whoever has will be given more; whoever does not have, even what he thinks he has will be taken from him." (LK 8:17–18)

When Jesus mentions "having" in these places, he isn't talking about material things. He is referring to spiritual growth, which from his perspective is the one thing worth having.

Jesus told us about the tremendous size of the afterlife. He told us about our eternal progress. He even told us that our loved ones would create after-death homes for us, and would meet us at our deaths and take us there.

"In my father's house are many rooms; if it were not so, I would have told you. I am going there to prepare a place for you. And if I go and prepare a place for you, I will come back and take you to be with me that you also may be where I am. You know the way to the place where I am going." (JN 14:2–4)

"Blessed are the poor in spirit, for theirs is the kingdom of heaven. ... Blessed are the pure in heart, for they will see God." (MT 5:3, 8)

His Teachings Are a Prescription for Spiritual Advancement

The law of spiritual advancement is implacable. Contrary to modern Christian teachings about "salvation" resulting from the death of Jesus, Jesus himself is exactly right: there are no shortcuts. Much of what Jesus says in the Gospels can be read as lessons in better controlling your mind.

"Do not resist an evil person. If someone strikes you on the right cheek, turn to him the other also. And if someone wants to sue you and take your tunic, let him have your cloak as well. If someone forces you to go one mile, go with him two miles." (MT 5:39–41)

"You have heard that it was said to the people long ago, 'Do not murder, and anyone who murders will be subject to judgment.' But I tell you that anyone who is angry with his brother will be subject to judgment. Again, anyone who says to his brother, 'Raca,' is answerable to the Sanhedrin. But anyone who says, 'You fool' will be in danger of the fire of Gehenna." (MT 5:21–22)

"Why do you look at the speck of sawdust in your brother's eye and pay no attention to the plank in your own eye? How can you say to your brother, 'Brother, let me take the speck out of your eye,' when you yourself fail to see the plank in your own eye? You hypocrite, first take the plank out of your eye, and then you will see clearly to remove the speck from your brother's eye." (LK 6:41–42)

"If any one of you is without sin, let him be the first to throw a stone at her." (JN 8:7)

"But love your enemies, do good to them, and lend to them without expecting to get anything back. Then your reward will be great, and you will be sons of the Most High, because he is

kind to the ungrateful and wicked. Be merciful, just as your Father is merciful." (LK 6:35–36)

Jesus shared wonderful parables about spiritual growth. We know them as the tales of the Good Samaritan, the Keeper of the Vineyard, and the Prodigal Son. In every way that he could, he urged his listeners to keep striving for spiritual perfection.

"I tell you that in the same way there is more rejoicing in heaven over one sinner who repents than over ninety-nine righteous persons who do not need to repent." (LK 15:7)

He Did Not Like Clergymen or Religious Traditions

Jesus was kind to everyone. He loved even lepers and tax collectors, at a time when lepers were shunned by all and tax collectors were evil incarnate. The only people who griped him were clergymen. He was bothered by not just their fake piety and self-importance, but also their religious traditions.

"Watch out for the teachers of the law. They like to walk around in flowing robes and be greeted in the marketplaces, and have the most important seats in the synagogues and the places of honor at banquets. They devour widows' houses and for a show make lengthy prayers. Such men will be punished most severely." (MK 12:38–40)

"And why do you break the command of God for the sake of your tradition? … You hypocrites! Isaiah was right when he prophesied about you: 'These people honor me with their lips, but their hearts are far from me. They worship me in vain; their teachings are but rules taught by men.'" (MT 15:3–9)

"You have let go of the commands of God and are holding on to the traditions of men . . . You have a fine way of setting aside the

commands of God in order to observe your own traditions." (MK 7:8–9)

"Be careful not to do your 'acts of righteousness' before men, to be seen by them. If you do, you will have no reward from your Father in heaven. So when you give to the needy, do not announce it with trumpets, as the hypocrites do in the synagogues and on the streets, to be honored by men. I tell you the truth, they have received their reward in full. But when you give to the needy, do not let your left hand know what your right hand is doing, so that your giving may be in secret. Then your father, who sees what is done in secret, will reward you. When you pray, do not be like the hypocrites, for they love to pray standing in the synagogues and on the street corners to be seen by men. I tell you the truth, they have received their reward in full. When you pray, go into your room, close the door and pray to your Father, who is unseen. Then your Father, who sees what is done in secret, will reward you." (MT 6:1–6)

Does this sound like someone who was trying to establish his own religion? Or was he instead telling us that we don't need religions at all, but we can approach God individually, since each of us is part of universal Mind? Jesus's teachings are profoundly individual.

"Ask, and it will be given to you; seek, and you will find; knock, and the door will be opened to you. For everyone who asks receives; he who seeks finds; and to him who knocks, the door is opened." (LK 11:9–10)

"Not everyone who says to me, 'Lord, Lord,' will enter the kingdom of heaven, but only he who does the will of my Father who is in heaven." (MT 7:21)

"Why do you call me 'Lord, Lord,' and not do what I say?" (LK 6:46)

"If you hold to my teaching, you are really my disciples. Then you will know the truth, and the truth will set you free." (JN 8:31–32)

It amazes me that so little has been made of the fact that this perfectly loving man seems to have had an aversion to religions. Does it not seem possible that, far from establishing yet one more religion, Jesus was trying to "set you free" from religions altogether?

His Death Was Not Meant to Save Us from God's Wrath

I have a confession to make. I have always found it hard to believe that a perfectly loving God would demand the blood-sacrifice of His own child. Whenever I asked clergymen about it, they would say it was "a sacred mystery." I know better now. **The afterlife evidence tells us that accepting Jesus as one's personal savior is not necessary for salvation, and neither God nor any religious figure ever is our afterlife judge.** So if Jesus didn't die as a blood-sacrifice to redeem us from God's punishment for our sins, then what else might have been the purpose of his dramatic death and resurrection?

Perhaps it was an exclamation point. Perhaps he was demonstrating for simple people the good news that death is not real.

Jesus's Message Is Not That Being a Christian Is the Only Way to Salvation

As Christianity developed, Christians became convinced that Jesus had said that accepting him as one's personal savior was the only way to heaven.

"I am the way, the truth and the life. No one comes to the Father except through me." (JN 14:6)

"I am the resurrection and the life. He who believes in me will live, even though he dies; and whoever lives and believes in me will never die." (JN 11:25–26)

Afterlife evidence does not support this Christians-only reading of his words, but it would support another reading. Simply replace "I" and "me" with "my teachings":

"My teachings are the way, the truth and the life. No one comes to the Father except through my teachings."

"My teachings are the resurrection and the life. He who believes in my teachings will live, even though he dies; and whoever lives and believes in my teachings will never die."

Jesus so persistently emphasized our need to follow *his teachings* that this revised reading makes more sense. Perhaps those who heard him misunderstood him, or perhaps later custodians of his words altered them to better support developing Christian doctrines. Unfortunately, in reliance on those altered words, Jesus's followers soon were torturing and murdering and committing mayhem in his name, in utter contravention of his teachings. No conversion effort has been considered too brutal to be used, if making people Christian was the only way to "save" them.

But Jesus told us repeatedly that *following his teachings* is what matters!

"What do you think? There was a man who had two sons. He went to the first and said, 'Son, go and work today in the vineyard.' 'I will not,' he answered, but later he changed his mind and went. Then the father went to the other son and said the same thing. He answered, 'I will, sir,' but he did not go. Which of the two did what his father wanted? . . . I tell you the truth, the tax collectors and the prostitutes are entering the kingdom of God ahead of you." (MT 21:28–31)

"I say to you that many will come from the east and the west, and will take their places at the feast with Jacob in the kingdom of heaven. But the subjects of the kingdom will be thrown outside, into the darkness, where there will be weeping and gnashing of teeth." (MT 8:11–12)

Most comforting of all his words are these:

"I shall be with you always, to the very end of the age." (MT 28:20)

What Was His Mission?

Jesus was speaking to primitive people steeped in superstitious terrors and ignorant of nearly everything that you and I consider commonplace. His teachings for them were simple, even simplistic. We severely underestimate the man if we suppose that if he walked the earth today, he would express himself to us as he expressed himself to them. If we keep this fact in mind, then in light of modern afterlife evidence we can develop a pretty good sense of what Jesus was trying to do.

I think Jesus's life had a four-fold purpose.

First, he came to tell us what God is.

Second, he came to show us that life is eternal.

Third, he came to give us a taste of what the afterlife is like.

Finally, he came to teach us how to make the most spiritual progress while on Earth.

If these were his objectives, then his death and resurrection can be seen as a loving and joyous "Ta-da!"

At last, two thousand years ago, human beings were ready to start to learn what modern afterlife evidence has only now revealed to us, two very bloody millennia later. Had his followers fully understood what he was saying at the time, human history could have been so different!

Mainstream Christianity does not own Jesus, just as no religion owns God. Surely he deserves another chance to be heard in light of modern afterlife evidence. Paul and the other New Testament writers did a good job of wrapping Jesus's teachings in Hebrew prophesy so they could be preserved for two thousand years. **Thank you, Paul! Now at last we can open your gift.**

Appendix IV
A Brief Overview of the Afterlife Evidence

We have nearly two hundred years of astonishingly varied afterlife evidence. And just as important as the volume and variety of this evidence is the fact that it is so consistent, and when we put it all together we begin to glimpse a wonderfully complex and beautiful reality that dwarfs the material universe. Indeed, the greater reality now coming into view might be as much as twenty times the size of our universe! It is all beyond amazing, and far beyond thrilling.

I recommend that you read Victor and Wendy Zammit's important book, *A Lawyer Presents the Evidence for the Afterlife*, and that you also peruse some of the seventy-odd books listed in the Appendix II annotated bibliography. To help you get started, I will here list in no particular order some of the kinds of evidence that I have used in assembling my understanding of death, the afterlife, and the greater reality in which we live:

Communications Received Through Deep-Trance Mediums. Deep-trance mediums are able to withdraw from their bodies sufficiently to let the dead use their vocal cords to speak. The testimony of the best evidence received this way is such that if mainstream physicists had not a century ago already been dogmatically materialist, the fact that you will survive your death would long ago have become common knowledge.

Communications Received Through Materialization Mediums. There are mediums who have developed their skills to such an extent that they can go into deep trance and facilitate the production of voices, sounds, and even our loved ones physically present in the room.

Communications Received Through Psychic Mediums. This is an area where double- and triple-blind scientific studies are possible, and these studies demonstrate that some psychic mediums indeed are in contact with the dead. The work of the best psychic mediums has produced a wealth of interesting and consistent information.

Accounts Received Through Automatic Writing. Sometimes a medium can invite a dead person to write using the medium's hands. I have read a few accounts that were written this way, and have found them to be so consistent with the information that I have assembled from other sources that I consider the ones that I have read to be likely genuine.

Channeled Accounts. Throughout history, there have been mediums who have received in one way or another entire books that they claimed came from dead people, and that purportedly gave us the straight skinny on what is really going on. I have mistrusted most channeled work, so it is a humbling irony that I have lately been made to understand that all my books have been channeled. Never say that God doesn't have a sense of humor.

Consciousness Research. A century ago, mainstream physicists still grappling with quantum mechanics considered the proofs of their survival that the dead had begun to send to us to be a woo-woo bridge too far. In order to be able to ignore the dead, university departments and peer-reviewed journal gatekeepers established materialism as what they called a "fundamental scientific dogma." To this day, no research scientist who hopes for a university career dares to study anything that might suggest that reality is based in an underlying intelligence. As a result, researchers still labor in vain to find a source of consciousness inside the brain. What bits of information they produce are studied by afterlife researchers, but in truth we are coming to know a lot more about consciousness than they do.

Deathbed Visions. Those who are dying will often have extraordinary experiences that include visits from dead loved ones and occasional glimpses of the places where they will be going after death.

Accounts by Out-of-Body Travelers. There is a lot of evidence that we travel out of our bodies during sleep, but to learn to do it while awake is difficult. There are some, though, who have demonstrated an ability to travel out of their bodies at will, and the published accounts by out-of-body travelers are remarkably consistent with the rest of the evidence.

General Scientific Research. From enigmas like dark matter and energy and the Big Bang, right through to the troubling fact that "solid" matter is not solid, modern scientific inquiry remains severely hamstrung by its obsession with materialism as a dogma. At the same time, scientific researchers continue to turn out consistent bits of information that help afterlife researchers as we build our increasingly detailed picture of the greater reality.

Ghosts and Spirit Possession. These are areas so repugnant to me that I try not even to think about them, but little by little I have felt forced to investigate the phenomena of ghosts and spirit possession. And, yes, what we are learning there fits the overall picture that we are building.

Hypnotic Regression and Progression. Some therapists help their patients regress or progress to what appear to be past or future lives, and thereby help them to resolve some psychological ailments. In doing so, they have uncovered some fascinating, and consistent, information.

Instrumental Transcommunication (ITC) Including Electronic Voice Phenomena (EVP). Communicating with the dead by means of computers, tape recorders, telephones, televisions, and various "black box" devices is a very promising area that has yet to bear much fruit, in part because few living researchers are able to devote the necessary time to conducting experiments at the direction of dead researchers. And occasionally, squabbling among living researchers will cause their dead collaborators to withdraw. More recently, we have come to understand that there also are some very bad nonmaterial entities who are trying to keep reliable communication between the living and the dead from ever happening. Knowing what is wrong is half of solving the problem. Expect reliable electronic communication with the dead to be in place before 2030.

Near-Death Experiences. We are told by those that we used to think were dead that people who have near-death experiences don't go to the places where the dead reside, but they generally travel out of their bodies and they often have remarkable experiences. When we understand that the events depicted in near-death experiences are not indicative of afterlife facts, we can study just the mechanics of NDEs. And there we find information that is entirely consistent with what we have learned from other sources.

Past-Life Memories of Children. Some toddlers appear to have memories of recent past lives that ended violently. These cases seem to me to be less evidence for general reincarnation than they are suggestions of what might perhaps go wrong in the process of transition.

Quantum Physics. The physics of the places where the dead reside is so different from the physics of this level of reality that until good quantum-physics-for-dummies books became available early in this century, afterlife researchers had trouble making sense of it all. It turns out that quantum physics is a kind of plug that connects what we might think of as the mathematics-based physics of this level of reality with the consciousness-based physics that exists in perhaps ninety-five percent of the greater reality that even physicists are aware must exist. Thanks to those who have made the principles of quantum mechanics understandable to people who never got beyond Algebra II, afterlife researchers are coming to understand a lot more about how reality is put together.

Work of Independent Scientists. Nearly all researchers in the field of afterlife studies are lawyers, psychologists, and other laypeople. We revere those few trained scientists who during the past century have come across data that suggested there was a lot more going on than what was currently being studied. And despite the strong stigma in scientific circles that still exists against scientists who don't respect the "fundamental dogma of materialism," and despite the lack of funding for researchers who venture off the materialist reservation, a few of these visionaries have done extraordinary work in fields related to afterlife studies. All such research results of which I am aware are consistent with what has been developed by earnest laypeople.

Appendix V
A Brief Overview of the Greater Reality

What afterlife researchers have discovered is a lot more than just the happy fact that every human mind is eternal. Because the afterlife is real, our study of it has led us to the amazing discovery of a greater reality that seems to be many times the size of this material universe, and to a new kind of physics that is consciousness-based. To give you even a rudimentary understanding of the whole picture would take a separate book. Here, I will just share with you brief descriptions of some of the aspects of the afterlife on which researchers generally agree.

God

No human-like God exists. Instead, the only thing that exists is an energy-like potentiality without size or form, infinitely powerful, alive in the sense that your mind is alive, highly emotional and therefore probably self-aware. And the only emotion this genuine God expresses is love beyond our ability to comprehend it. Each human mind is part of God. It is likely not wrong to say that God and all our minds together are of an energy that we experience as consciousness, but no one knows much about God beyond the definition given above. Everything that we think of as real is an aspect or an artifact of God. And creation, if you want to call it that, is apparently not a one-time thing. Evidence suggests that God is continuously manifesting the reality that we believe exists around us.

The Structure of the Greater Reality

The simplest way to envision reality is as a spectrum of energy signals very much like the television signals that are in the room around you, and to imagine your mind as a television set now tuned to that particular body on this material level of reality. We think this is the lowest vibratory level, but no one is sure about that. We do know that existing at slightly higher vibratory rates are at least seven levels of nonmaterial reality that include our afterlife levels. Each of them may be as big as this whole material universe; and all of them, like the TV signals in the room around you, are together in one place.

Nothing is solid. Everything is energy. The only thing that objectively exists is God, and every human mind is an infinitely loved part of God.

The Afterlife Levels

There are at least seven primary energy-based post-death levels of reality, each of them containing what are apparently almost infinite sub-levels. Six of those primary levels can feel as solid to their inhabitants as this material level feels to us, and all of them are in the same place, just as you can tune your TV from a lower channel to a higher channel and find there a different TV program. We can be comfortable on the highest afterlife level to which our personal degree of spiritual development suits us, but we find it unbearable to go higher. And we want to go higher! There is more to do, there are ever more pleasures on the higher vibratory levels. So the more spiritual progress you can make in this lifetime, the more kinds of fun will be available to you later.

Right above the vibratory rate of matter is the lowest afterlife level, what Jesus called the outer darkness. It is the punishment level, cold and dark, smelly and repellent and populated by tormented, demon-like people; and the evidence indicates that everyone who is there essentially has put himself there. We have found no evidence of any post-death judgment by anyone but ourselves.

Just above the lowest primary afterlife level is a recovery level, still twilight-dark, but with homes and without the awful cold and stench and hopelessness of the lowest level.

Levels Three through Five of the afterlife are the beautiful Summerland levels. All three are intensely earthlike, full of enormous flowers in extraordinary colors and magnificent buildings and scenery. The higher the vibratory rate of each of these levels, the more gorgeous everything appears to be.

Primary Level Six is just below the Source. Historically the dead have called it the causal or mental level, since it is the home of spiritually advanced people who mind-create what exists in the lower afterlife levels. (I recall long ago reading an account from a sixth-level being who was frustrated by the process of learning how to create living plants. It was hilarious.) A friend of mine who died in 2007 and now lives in the sixth level refers to it as the teaching level, since for many who live at that level, spiritual teaching in the lower afterlife levels and on earth is a primary occupation. He tells us that Level Six is full of beautiful universities where very advanced beings help one another to make ever more spiritual progress.

The highest vibratory level of which we are aware is the Celestial or Source Level, which is something like the center of God. It exists at such a high spiritual vibratory rate that it seems that very few of us have yet been able to enter it. The Celestial Level is the source of the magnificent white light that fills most of the greater reality and makes it feel to those who are there as if they are living bathed in love.

The Death Process

Our bodies resist dying. Getting them to the point where they can no longer support life and we are released from these earthly shells can be a rough experience, as I have been reminded by some who objected to the title of my book, *The Fun of Dying*. But shortly before we leave our bodies, the fun begins as we start to see some of those we had loved in life and thought were dead come crowding around our deathbed. We leave our bodies as what might appear to bedside observers to be an energy mist, and we re-form into a human shape while still attached to our material body by a spiritual umbilicus called the silver cord. This process of liberation is quite pleasurable, as is our joyous reunion with loved ones at our bedside. We might hardly notice the fraying of our silver cord, but once it is severed, the physical body dies. Then we are off with those we love, raising our spiritual vibratory rate to the point where a whole new solid and beautiful reality appears around us. If you will trust in the process, you will find that dying is just that easy, and just that wonderful.

Our Post-Death Life

A whole book by itself could be written about all that the dead have been pleased to tell us about their wonderful post-death lives. Here are a few highlights:

Our bodies are mind-created, and most of us choose to look and feel as we did while on earth at maybe age thirty. The standard "spirit robe" is a long-sleeved, floor-length belted tunic in vibrant pastel hues, like an angel's dress; but many people prefer to wear earth-clothing. Nobody cares how you dress. My sixth-level friend who died in 2007 at the age of 20 tells us that he wears college-kid clothes most of the time, but when he returns to the sixth level he wears his spirit robe.

Dead children are treated like royalty, reared in beautiful homes and villages that are off-limits to any but their carefully-selected caretakers. They grow to young adulthood at their own pace, generally over just a few earth-years, and they closely follow their parents' lives and greet their eventual arrival with joy. Even miscarried and aborted babies grow up here and lovingly greet their parents. I recall reading one early-twentieth-century communication in which a woman who apparently had had several coat-hanger abortions reported having been staggered to be greeted by four beautiful young adults who loved her and called her their mother.

There are infinite things to do. And since night never falls and we don't need to sleep, we have close to infinite time in which to happily entertain ourselves. We travel in space and travel in time, play sports, learn to paint and play the piano, research our past lives, attend Elvis concerts, take classes, boat and fly around, show up at impromptu welcoming parties, and even sit at the feet of Jesus. My sixth-level friend spends a lot of time snowboarding. The more spiritually advanced you are, the more options are available to you, which is another reason to take your earthly spiritual growth seriously.

All the companion animals we have loved in life are there to greet us, now young and healthy. Most animals have species-specific "group souls" to which they return at death, but being loved by a human being enables them to establish an independent existence. They live in the afterlife in happy packs, or they live with your family members until you arrive. Like us, they neither eat nor eliminate, so the only care that they need now is love.

And yes, I do understand that all of this seems too good to be true. You are coming home hoping for milk and cookies and comfort after your rough day in school, and what you get instead is a three-ring circus of ponies and elephants and aerial acts and every earthly pleasure. As I have read so many wonderful accounts, sometimes I could envision the heavenly host sort of chortling together with glee as they thought up ever more treats that you in particular might enjoy. It is impossible for you to grasp the infinite extent to which you are perfectly loved.

Appendix VI
Experiences of Light

My lifelong interest in death is an offshoot of something that happened in April of 1955. One morning I woke up just before dawn and was struck by the thought that there is no God. I stared in terror into the darkness, too full of despair even to seek the comfort of my parents' bed. What comfort can there be if there is no God?

Suddenly there was a flash of white light in the room. I could look at it without squinting, and even more than sixty years later I still recall the wonder of seeing light shining on my toy horse, on my plastic dolls in a row, and on that awful lavender wallpaper. In the midst of the flash, I heard a young male voice say, **"You wouldn't know what it is to have me unless you knew what it is to be without me. I will never leave you again."**

Almost forty years went by before I told anyone what had happened to me, but that experience shaped my growing-up. Surely my experience of light had been normal. I assumed that I was going to learn about experiences of light at church or in school or somewhere. I even majored in religion in college, but of course all that I learned in college was what the world's great religions had taught. By my junior year, I was starting to think that my experience would be a mystery forever. Then, one August day as I was turning twenty, I came home from my summer job and sat down on my bed, feeling glum.

Suddenly there it was again, the magnesium-white light filling the room, this time accompanied by indescribable music. Think of a thousand tiny bells playing beautifully and loudly. Then came that same young male voice, this time saying only, **"I will never leave you."**

Never for a minute since that day have I thought that I was alone, and never have I doubted the existence of God. And for many years, I was convinced that I was the literal dunce of the universe, since God had to make His point to me twice. I was so embarrassed that for years I swore to God that I always would remember that He was real, **"so please don't ever do that to me again!"** In all the years since, God never has.

For nearly four decades I lived with the thought that the only three people who ever had been spoken to out of a flash of light were Moses, the Apostle Paul, and a dumbfounded American child.

Here is what happened to Moses:

"The angel of the Lord appeared to him in a blazing fire from the midst of a bush; and he looked, and behold, the bush was burning with fire, yet the bush was not consumed. So Moses said, **'I must turn aside now and see this marvelous sight, why the bush is not burned up.'**

"When the Lord saw that he turned aside to look, God called to him from the midst of the bush and said, **'Moses, Moses!'**

"And he said, **'Here I am.'**

"Then He said, **'Do not come near here; remove your sandals from your feet, for the place on which you are standing is holy ground'"** (Exodus 3:2–5).

And here is how a zealot named Saul was converted after the death of Jesus from a persecutor of those who had followed the Lord into the Apostle Paul, the architect of the early Church:

"Now Saul, still breathing threats and murder against the disciples of the Lord, went to the high priest, and asked for letters from him to the synagogues at Damascus, so that if he found any belonging to the Way, both men and women, he might bring them bound to Jerusalem. As he was traveling, it happened that he was approaching Damascus, and suddenly a light from heaven flashed around him; and he fell to the ground and heard a voice saying to him, **'Saul, Saul, why are you persecuting Me?'**

"And he said, **'Who are You, Lord?'**

"And He said, **'I am Jesus whom you are persecuting, but get up and enter the city, and it will be told you what you must do'**" (Acts 9:1–6).

These great religious figures had conversed with the voices they had heard from the light. For my part, when I saw the light and heard the voice, my only thought was that it was handy that if you forget there is a God, they remind you. But until I was forty-five, I never heard of anyone else outside the Bible who had had an experience of light.

Then my father had a major stroke. For the two weeks that he survived, I made a daily round trip to be with my parents, and on one of those nights my mother had essentially my same experience. She saw a flash of white light, and a voice said, **"I'm giving you a few more days with him so you can get a few things straight."**

(Nobody said these great experiences have to be poetic.)

It was only after I discovered that they had not been unique to me that I began to mention my experiences of light. I have found that a few of those with whom I have shared my experiences have had similar experiences themselves, and they generally don't talk about them, either. This is something so personal, so extraordinary, and frankly so weird that you don't talk about it. But it is something that stays in your mind. I have no other memories from the spring when I was eight, but still that predawn minute shines.

As to what makes an experience of light look and sound as it does, here are my thoughts:

- All the post-death levels exist right here, and the third level and above are filled with a white light that is brighter than sunlight. Opening a portal between our levels might leak that light through briefly, which I have come to think is what happens.
- Most people who have experiences of light have the same sense that I did: the light is in the room, but the voice and music may be in your mind.
- Experiences of light seem to occur when we are under some spiritual strain, and most of the messages that have been shared with me were spiritual in nature.
- People differ on who it was they thought they heard speaking, and by their descriptions I have come to guess that we all hear different voices. The voice that I heard was young and male and it didn't seem quite God-like, so when in my research I encountered spirit guides, I realized that my voice must have been my spirit guide. My mother was certain that she had heard the literal

voice of God Himself, and I find it interesting that as her brain deteriorated with end-stage senile dementia, her experience of light was the last thing she forgot, even when she no longer recognized her children.
- To hear a voice in your mind as clearly as you hear spoken words is a remarkable experience. I assure you that you can tell the difference between spoken words and your own thoughts. No question.

Having lived successfully for decades after I had my last experience of light, having married and reared children and practiced law and made friends, I am demonstrably not crazy. But I am so glad that at the age of eight I knew enough not to tell anyone what had happened to me! Now I wonder how many others have been made to consider themselves insane because they had this sort of wonderful cross-dimensional message, and the doctors they trusted with it decided that they had to be mad. I have come to think that many things that mainstream scientists still find puzzling may have their origins in the afterlife levels, which is another reason why I hope that soon they can get past their beliefs-based views of what reality must be.

www.ingramcontent.com/pod-product-compliance
Lightning Source LLC
Chambersburg PA
CBHW071834080526
44589CB00012B/1005